getting naked

getting naked

The Quiet Work of Becoming Perfectly Imperfect

VALERIE BERTINELLI

HARPER WAVE
An Imprint of HarperCollinsPublishers

Excerpts from "Instructions for a Body" courtesy of Marty McConnell.

Without limiting the exclusive rights of any author, contributor or the publisher of this publication, any unauthorized use of this publication to train generative artificial intelligence (AI) technologies is expressly prohibited. HarperCollins also exercise their rights under Article 4(3) of the Digital Single Market Directive 2019/790 and expressly reserve this publication from the text and data mining exception.

GETTING NAKED. Copyright © 2026 by Tuxedo Ltd. All rights reserved. No part of this book may be used or reproduced in any manner whatsoever without written permission except in the case of brief quotations embodied in critical articles and reviews. For information, address HarperCollins Publishers, 195 Broadway, New York, NY 10007. In Europe, HarperCollins Publishers, Macken House, 39/40 Mayor Street Upper, Dublin 1, D01 C9W8, Ireland.

HarperCollins books may be purchased for educational, business, or sales promotional use. For information, please email the Special Markets Department at SPsales@harpercollins.com.

hc.com

FIRST EDITION

Designed by Tai Blanche
All photos courtesy of the author
Frame graphics © Tuesday04/stock.adobe.com

Library of Congress Cataloging-in-Publication Data has been applied for.

ISBN 978-0-06-342908-6

Printed in the United States of America

25 26 27 28 29 LBC 5 4 3 2 1

To my son.
You shine in my heart like the moon and the stars and have expanded any limit I thought my heart could possibly hold. Life isn't perfect and that's okay because love always gets us through.

All is well. Everything is working out for my highest good. Out of this situation only good will come. I am safe.

—LOUISE HAY

There's more than one answer to these questions pointing me in a crooked line

—INDIGO GIRLS, "CLOSER TO FINE"

I'm doing the best I can and I can always do better.

—DBT MANTRA

contents

introduction: the poetry of being............................ xi

WALKING 1
MY ROOTS ARE SHOWING 15
PUZZLES 29
CLIMATE CHANGE 49
DRY JANUARY, FEBRUARY ... DECEMBER, AND BEYOND 63
in a warm bath (a meditation)............................ 80
JUST BREATHE 85
FALLING 97
IF I COULD TALK TO MY ANIMALS (AND IF THEY COULD TALK TO ME) 109
GETTING NAKED 123
sitting still with anger and disappointment (a meditation)...... 138
SMALLER AND WISER 143
NEVER SAY NEVER 155
CONNECTIONS 171
AND YET 181
healing (a meditation)................................... 190
TIME (DON'T HURRY, BE HAPPY) 195
GOOD WORK 203
A PARTING THOUGHT 215

acknowledgments 220

introduction

THE POETRY OF BEING

*Our job is to learn and to love,
and I want to be better at it.
I want to be better.*

JOURNAL ENTRY, JULY 2024

STRIP EVERYTHING AWAY. *All of it. Physically, mentally, and emotionally. Take off the clothes. Don't suck in the gut. Drop the facade. Stop pretending. Get rid of the chains. No judging, no making faces, no regrets. Stand there and look, really look . . . and feel what it feels like.*

I take it all in—the chill of the air on my naked body, the wrinkles, the sagging skin, the messy bed-hair with roots showing, the parts of me that I cover up, the fear of letting it out, the shame, the "Do Not Open" label on the box of secrets I have kept; but also, there's the strength in my arms and legs, this body that gave birth to a new life, that feels desire, vulnerability, hunger, courage, humor, acceptance, curiosity, connection . . . the breaths filling my lungs, my beating heart, my love, my mortality, my humanity . . . this moment, right now.

Breathe. Find the love.

Feel the love. With each breath, with each heartbeat, feel the love.

It sounds like a poem. Because it is poetry. I would hope it is to all of us. It should be. It is life, our life, in all its glorious, imperfect, and irresistible potential. It's what I told myself, what I saw, and what I felt when I stepped in front of the full-length mirror in my bathroom sometime after my sixty-fourth birthday—and my reaction surprised me.

I had thought I was almost done with my healing journey, and to some degree I was. If I had stopped where I was, I would have been fine, grateful for my health and well-being and everything else in my life. My knees ached when I climbed the stairs to my bedroom, but hey, welcome to your Medicare years. And I woke up in a mood some days for reasons I couldn't figure out. But who doesn't feel that way occasionally, with all that's going on in the world, with all the complications and pressures on our shoulders, with all the bad news and yelling on TV?

Except I was not at peace with myself, not the way I imagined being at this age, after all the work I'd done on myself. I could feel unease just under my skin as well as other things going on at depths where it was too dark to see. I'd been through a lot professionally and personally. Death. Divorce. Job loss. Money issues. Health concerns. Who isn't going through something big?

I thought I was handling things. Sure, I had cried my eyes out on more than a few occasions. I had spent too many hours sitting in a dark corner of my office feeling scared of whatever might come next. And there were those days when I was just too exhausted to get out of my pj's and face the world.

Of course, there were also periods when I felt great, where I not only reminded myself to stop and smell the roses, I did it. Literally. I walked outside and smelled the roses in my yard. But overall I was just out of . . . well, I'm guessing you know the indescribable thing that I was out of and that's no way to feel. No way to live.

My realization? I had more work to do. It wasn't exactly a joyous epiphany. I had spent the past decade going through what I'll call the six stages of trying to love myself: (1) judgment, (2) dieting, (3) frustration, (4) more dieting and exhaustion (diets don't work), (5) healthy acceptance (my body isn't the problem)—and now I was at the sixth and last stage: Shit, I have more work to do.

As I said, this came as a surprise to me. It shouldn't have. Who doesn't have more work to do? Growth, understanding, the quest for equanimity—finding calm and clarity in my chaos—is a process. Finding love, allowing yourself to be loved, and being able to feel that love seep and sit inside you . . . being able to see and understand and accept the whole, the good and the bad, the laughter and the tears, the ups and the downs as one, as the poetry of being, of our being. It's all a lifelong process. And that is the point I've learned to keep in mind.

I have this theory that we have multiple voices in our head, and mine talk to me all the time. Some are serious, some are childlike, some are scolding, some are downright silly. As I ventured into sixty-four, one voice was saying, "You've come a long way, baby," and another was asking, "Are you done with falling in love?" Another whispered, "Psst, remember that thing that happened when you were a little girl? Do you want to finally talk about it?" And still another was reminding me that I had leftover steak in the fridge. It's a jumble up there, like morning traffic on the 405.

Several of those voices reminded me that I had set up some emotional guardrails for myself that I had yet to dismantle. *Shit, I have more work to do.* It was a little shocking and unsettling, and, frankly speaking, it caught me unprepared. Hadn't I been through enough? Love, loss, marriage, and divorce—twice! The weight loss, the weight gain, getting on the scale, off the scale, public scrutiny, understanding there is no magic number. My parents were both gone. My son was married. I had already issued a declaration to myself, the world, other women, and God herself: Enough already!

But no, apparently it wasn't enough.

The voices were talking to me: "You need to get acquainted with the self-loathing you feel so deeply inside. You need to be conscious of the darkness. You need to find a way to understand and let go of the anger you're carrying around. Sit beside it. Get curious. Don't be afraid. You need to let yourself be vulnerable. You need to let yourself have a good cry for that little girl who never allowed herself to feel.

You need to laugh. Within all that, you will find yourself. You will stop thinking of the past and the future and settle into a comfortable place within yourself, in the present."

I did something new and different from the past. I paid attention to those voices and listened to what they were telling me. Sometimes I said, "What?" Other times I groaned, "Are you kidding me?" Ultimately, I got to a place where I was saying, "You're right. Tell me more." And gradually I found myself doing what they were telling me. Out of necessity. Out of love. For my health and quality of life.

It became a journey I was not aware that I was on and it's now this book. The stories comprise a panorama of reflection and self-discovery. Sketches of everyday vulnerability lead into not-so-everyday confrontations with truths about myself that needed, finally, to happen. It's about being honest, fearless, vulnerable. It's about peeling back the layers of protection and avoidance I had worn for most of my life. It's about stepping into the shadows, opening doors, turning on lights, and facing a past too long considered off-limits, and saying to yourself, "Yeah, this happened. It was bad. It's held me hostage long enough. It's time to finally deal and move forward." It's about freeing myself from the emotional restraints of trauma, shame, and guilt. It's about feeling hope and finding love. It's about getting naked so I could see myself, all of me, and finally like what I see.

I know some people will read this and say, "Oh, shut up, you poor spoiled thing." And I get it. I hear you and acknowledge your opinion. But I know there are many more who are like me, fighting internal battles, carrying around secrets that no one sees, wishing the past could be rewritten because of the way it colors the present, and even more so, wanting a way to simply and finally move on and be ourselves, our whole selves, our full and beautiful and loving selves.

If you're reading this book, I have a sense that you and I are pretty similar. We aren't crushable. We are the opposite, in fact; we are people who are striving for a rich, whole, fulfilling life. We are thinkers. We are sensitive. We feel deeply. We have faced challenges and collected our share of bruises. We have kept quiet about things until we have found it impossible to keep quiet any longer. We want to like ourselves. No, we want to love ourselves, and we want to be loved and return love vulnerably and safely. We want to experience the poetry of being, not avoid it.

Everything we've been through has put us on a path toward who we are, and I have found, or I should say, I am finding, we are a lot better, stronger, braver, and loving than we let ourselves believe—at least that's what I am discovering about myself. That's what I have written about this time around. How I got to the poetry of being.

I'm remembering one Sunday when I read a story in *The New York Times Magazine* by journalist-novelist Taffy Brodesser-Akner. She wrote about a family friend who had been kidnapped when she was young. The incident had inspired her latest novel. In the magazine story she explored the legacy of that family friend's trauma. It brought out memories of her own trauma. I won't go into any more detail. You can read it for yourself if you're interested—and may I suggest you do, because it is beautifully written. But she wrote something in particular that I found profoundly insightful and true about dealing with trauma:

INTRODUCTION

After all your attempts at healing—when you finally realize that you are forever changed—you can allow yourself to embrace your trauma. You survive what happened to you, then you survive your survival,* and then the gift you're given is that you fall in love with your whole life, inextricable from the bad thing that happened to you.

Amen.
Now, let's get naked.

---

* *Then you survive your survival.* My God. That phrase alone stopped me in my tracks. Exquisite.

walking

When in doubt, send love.
Never suppress a generous thought.

JOURNAL ENTRY, DECEMBER 2023

"I DON'T KNOW if she'll be able to walk again. If she does, it will be a long while before that happens. Right now she's lucky to be alive."

That was my friend telling me that his wife, one of my best friends, was in the hospital, in serious condition, after being hit by a car while crossing the street. She was, indeed, lucky to be alive. But she was going to live. Would she walk again? That was to be determined—and it was something that lodged itself in my brain in the days and weeks after I received that stunning news.

At the time, I was in the habit of walking on my treadmill every day—or at least thinking about it. *Gotta get in my steps!* That was in addition to all the walking I did in the course of my day. I walked countless times from my kitchen up a flight of stairs to my office. I walked back downstairs to make a cup of coffee. I walked to the bathroom. I walked around the kitchen when I made lunch and dinner. I walked quickly down the driveway to catch the delivery guy to tell him that the package he had given me was for someone down the street. I walked through airports, into hotels, and through the streets of New York City to get to the set of *The Drew Barrymore Show*.

I walked all day and some of the night until I got into bed. I probably walked in my dreams, but I don't remember.

I wasn't particularly mindful of it as I went about my day. I did think about my girlfriend at least a thousand times a day, each thought accompanied by a deep shudder weighted with concern and love, the fragility of life and the way luck—or bad luck—can change everything we take for granted in an instant.

Would she walk again?

One minute she was sharing dessert with her husband, the next he was holding her hand in the back of an ambulance.

I vaguely remember when my son took his first steps. What I recall was the excitement. "He walked!" I told Ed. I told my parents. Ed told his brother. It was as if a switch was flipped and my son went from crawling and falling to walking and falling to getting on with the rest of his life. Baby steps. That's the way I started to walk, according to my mom—and the way everyone starts, I suppose. One step, another, then a wobble, and kaboom, down we go. We pull ourselves along, then let go. Muscle strength, balance, coordination—it all comes together. It's not even a conscious decision. It really is like a switch is flipped. One day you can walk.

Then, suddenly, you're a toddler—and off you go, toddling along, as I have done for the rest of my life. Toddling with a bottle in your hand, and later in life a glass of wine. If life had a speed limit, I think toddling would be perfect. My friend had to relearn how to toddle. However, before that, she had to regain muscle strength, coordination, and balance. She was back to baby steps, taking them with desire and determination, with intention and purpose.

I pictured my friend in rehab as Wonder Woman. Her effort to return to life as she knew it was nothing short of heroic. It filled me with awe. I could easily choke up thinking about this grown woman who drove carpools with me, who showed up every Wednesday together with me to assist the teacher while our boys were in kindergarten, and who cried next to me as her husband officiated my son's wedding and her son served as one of the best men. She and her husband had just spent three months in Italy, returned home, and then a car turning the corner struck her cold. That kind of stuff is hidden in the smallest of fine print of life's instruction manual.

Her situation caused me to think about walking, the literal importance of walking, in my life, which sounds peculiar if not totally banal. There is profundity, after all, in something as simple as putting one foot before the other. Going somewhere. Moving forward. Just moving! And, getting from point A to point B is the story of my life. I started thinking things like: "Am I walking purposely? Aimlessly? Am I walking to create a new path? Or am I walking to avoid something unpleasant? Am I walking with the universe? Or am I walking in shame? Are my eyes looking forward? Or are they pointed down? Am I going in the right direction? Have I even thought about which direction I'm walking?"

Why had I not been thinking about these things?

* * *

Walking requires us to make choices. It gives us direction, whether we realize it or not. Walking is how we create a path into the future, into whatever and wherever is next. Walking is how we get home.

The truth is, I wasn't walking, and when you don't walk, you don't go anywhere. You stagnate. I was definitely stagnating.

In those years after the COVID nightmare, I was shut down personally and professionally. My second marriage was over and proceeding through the cesspool of legalese that results in divorce. Every day was a boxing lesson in which I felt like I was the punching bag. My Emmy-winning cooking series was canceled. A TV pilot I worked on was not picked up by the network. I worried about money. I wondered what, if anything, was next. I was plagued by recurring bad dreams at night. I listened to my cats purr. At least they loved me.

I asked myself how I had ended up alone at this stage of my life—and why. I was a good cook, I laughed easily, I looked pretty good in jeans and a T-shirt, I'm resilient and mostly easygoing. It truly doesn't take much to make me happy. And yet, like so many others, I was in a rut. I wasn't walking, I wasn't moving forward! I had to do something. I had to move. My back hurt, my neck had a permanent kink in it, and while I wasn't anywhere near my heaviest, I could feel the weight—the physical weight and the weight of the world—holding me down. I was doing a lot of googling then, mostly astrology charts and pop psychology disguised as ancient wisdom. *You are not a problem to fix. You are a work in progress.* Then one day I googled the health benefits of walking (it could just as easily been the health benefits of chocolate or red wine). I must've heard something on one of the talk shows about how easy it is to jump-start a new health regime or simply do yourself a favor by getting up off your ass and walking for twenty or thirty minutes every day. Or maybe it was a podcast. Or it might've been on TikTok.

It is possible to spend so much time self-helping on social media that there's no time to do the actual work. But the work is what I needed to do.*

I scrolled through a health-related site online that registered with me. Whether or not I was ready to admit it, I was in pain. If someone, say, my doctor, had asked where it hurt, I wouldn't have known where to point. I would've sounded like a twelve-year-old wanting to stay home from school: "It hurts everywhere." But I was intrigued. If walking could send oxygenated blood to the two most painful areas,

---

* It's been pointed out to me that some of us consume so much self-help content that we trick ourselves into thinking we did the work. Through our reposts and cut-and-pastes, we put ourselves in the position of content maker rather than viewer, only to find ourselves drawn back into the same content wheel over and over again, always setting goals but never doing the actual work. (Guilty as charged.)

my head and my heart, and decrease discomfort, I was in for at least thirty minutes a day. If it really worked, if I noticed an improvement, I might increase to an hour or more. I might even take up sleepwalking. I got excited. I was going to add this new activity to my day. Purpose. Intention. Mindfulness. Mindful walking. That would be it. I would walk my head and my heart back into a pain-free existence. Oxygenated blood would flow. The light would pour in. I got on the Google to see what the great, all-knowing, all-comforting Indian poet Rumi had to say about walking—and indeed the topic was covered in a quotation that's often attributed to Rumi, from the thirteenth century: "As you start to walk on the way, the way appears."

I believed him. I ordered new shoes from Kizik. The delivery guy walked them up my driveway and left them on my doorstep. Where they stayed for a day or two. Because I am one of the world's great procrastinators. Even though I told myself that I was going to start walking for my health, that I was going to walk until the fitness app on my Apple Watch filled with rings and lit up in attagirls and crazy-colored achievement badges, and even though the sun was shining as if calling my name like a girlfriend wanting to play, I didn't take that first step down the driveway.

Then one afternoon my dog, Luna, pointed her severe underbite and soulful brown eyes at me and said, "Hey, girl, how about taking me for a walk?"

I live in a houseful of cats and one dog, and all I'm going to say about that right now is, God bless dogs, especially my old girl.

At this point Luna had been living with me for about a decade. My former husband had wanted a dog, and despite being a lifelong cat person myself, I drove us to an adoption event at a local park and we picked out this cute little lady in need of serious orthodontics. I couldn't stop looking at her and vice versa. It was puppy love at first sight. She was almost a year old when she came home with us, and she grew into the best dog in the world. From day one, she knew to pee outside. She would pace in front of the back door until we noticed. She was also kind and sweet. She wanted attention in the gentlest way, and in a house run by cats, that was the way to be.

Probably because I am a cat lady, I never learned to initiate conversations with my pets. With cats, you only speak when spoken to or risk a look of impertinence that says, "Please, this is *my* time." Consequently, I never really talked to Luna the way most people talk to their dogs. I rarely walked by and said, "What's up?" I didn't ask if she wanted to play ball.* And I never paid much attention to the way she watched every move I made. I never took advantage of the quiet wisdom that dogs have, their ability to listen with deep interest to any thought or problem and respond with exactly the right answer: love. I never looked into her eyes and asked, "Do you know what's wrong with men?" And I didn't ask, "Hey, Luna, want to go for a walk?"

It took her a few years to ask me. I suppose she was like me in the sense that she wasn't in a hurry. She treated me with patience— perhaps too much patience, too much forgiveness. But once she posed the question, I got up, put on my new sneakers, and realized what dog owners everywhere know about their four-legged best friends: Next to putting out a bowl of fresh food or offering a between-meal treat, the way to make your pooch deliriously happy is to pick up their leash and walk toward the front door.

---

* Mainly because the first time I tried to play ball with her, she looked at the ball I had just thrown, then at me, as if I were crazy. "You want me to run after that? You threw it. You go get it." She had no interest in retrieving it. She still doesn't. She does love a good tug-of-war, though.

At around ten or eleven years old, Luna was about my age in dog years, but suddenly she was bouncing around like a puppy, as if she had springs in her paws. Her tail was wagging on automatic pilot. She looked at me as if I was the greatest human being on the planet. I had spent years searching for ways to find joy. Was this the secret? A collar, a leash, and a patch of grass outside to sniff and pee on.

She reminded me of the Jeff Spicoli character in *Fast Times at Ridgemont High* when he says to his teacher, "All I need are some tasty waves, a cool buzz, and I'm fine." All Luna needed was a walk through the neighborhood. The interesting thing, as I soon discovered, was that I needed it, too.

* * *

I once ran the Boston Marathon. I did it four days before I turned fifty. There were times when I was training when I wondered if I would make it to fifty. My heart never beat so hard or fast. My knees never ached like they did then. My feet hurt. My toes threatened to walk off the job. It was painful. I used to soak in my cold pool after long training sessions. The pain and the cold were an interesting combination, what I imagine it's like being brought back to life after a near-death experience.

People magazine's online headline said, "Valerie Bertinelli 'Euphoric' After Finishing Boston Marathon." Euphoric? I was delirious. I was also impressed with myself. Hell yeah. Running in general and especially running 26.2 miles is insane (and that last 0.2 is like, "Hello, are you effing kidding me?"). Traveling 26 miles is why Uber was invented. The shortest commercial flight in the US is 31 miles. Look it up. (Petersburg to Wrangell, Alaska.) So, running that distance? Unlike love, sex, and getting my nails done, once is enough.

But here's the best thing about a marathon. It's the athletic equivalent of garlic bread. Why? Because you know pasta will be coming next.

I had no idea where Luna was about to lead me. We walked out the front door, past the gate, down the driveway, and to the street, where we stopped. Luna looked up at me with an expression in her eyes that said, "Right or left? It doesn't matter to me." I don't remember which way we turned that day or the next or the day after that. Luna was right; it didn't matter whether we went right or left, only that we committed to a path and walked. The way would appear (thank you, Rumi).

Now, what I do remember about walking those first couple of weeks is how quickly it turned into a habit that made me almost as happy as Luna. I caught her eye, or she caught mine, then up we sprang, and before either of us could say, "Grab a sweater," we were headed toward the door. Two things happened. First, I left my earbuds at home. I had started out listening to music but within days realized I couldn't hear cars coming in either direction. And by the way, they drive fast. Way too fast in my neighborhood, if you ask me. And no one stops at stop signs anymore, which is another subject altogether—the slippage of little acts of decency and good behavior that make for the common good.

Anyway, without my earbuds, I heard the cars. Then I heard our footsteps. Then I heard the jinglejangle of Luna's tags. Then I heard the birds in the trees. Then I heard neighbors say hello to me. Then I heard my breathing, my heartbeat, and my thoughts. I could literally hear myself thinking. I could hear my voice—and not just the negative voices in my head. I had a voice. A real voice. But then all that was interrupted when I heard—

* * *

This is important. Some years before, I was on a walk with an old friend of mine who I loved but who had a tendency to be too frank. They stopped and said, "Do you hear that?" I looked around us, wondering what I was supposed to have heard. What did I miss? "Do you hear how your thighs are rubbing together when you walk?" they said. I could feel my face flush and I froze. I wanted to hide. No, I didn't hear my thighs rubbing together. And if I did or didn't, what did it matter?

This same friend also took the liberty to criticize my laugh as too loud. *I laughed too loud?* More and louder laughter is something the world needs. A laugh should not be stifled. The comment really got stuck in my head and took root. I started to stifle my laugh. A quiet laugh. Eventually there was no laugh at all. And after the walk that day, I went home and hid those workout pants in the back of my closet. I wish I hadn't done that. I wish I hadn't stifled my laugh. I wish I had turned to my friend and shrugged or laughed or said, "So what, Judgy McJudger. Why do you care?" People can be rude and hurtful, sometimes intentionally, sometimes from stupidity or thoughtlessness, and in hindsight, I don't have any hard feelings about that friend. Maybe they were just making a dumb observation. I don't know. What I do know is that the conversation I was having in my head was harsher than their comment. I was stuck in a bad place and that's why it hit so hard. Eventually, I had the common sense to end that friendship.

* * *

But back to the point I wanted to make. On one of those walks with Luna, I was wearing those same workout pants and heard my thighs rubbing together. I took a few more steps, then stopped. And started to giggle. "Did you hear that, Luna?" Either she didn't or she didn't care; I believe it was the latter. She tugged on the leash, eager to continue our walk. There was the sound again. My sound. The sound I seemed to make when I walked. That giggle turned into a chuckle, and then I laughed out loud, literally, emphasis on the loud.

Nobody was judging me. Nobody was criticizing me for something beyond my control. I wasn't judging myself, either. I didn't give a hoot if my thighs rubbed together and made a sound. This was a breakthrough!

I laughed again. I was taking care of myself, getting fresh air, and feeling the oxygenated blood going to my head and my heart.

When Luna and I first started, I thought our daily walks would be about me and my body and losing weight. If I did ten thousand steps, how could I miss getting in better shape, right? But soon, and without being conscious of the shift, I quit counting the number of steps I was logging and ceased to think about the weight I thought I wanted to lose. I left those concerns at home with my earbuds.

The walks, as advertised, were about my head and my heart. I let myself believe the birds were serenading me even though I knew they were gabbing among themselves.* I soaked up the breeze rustling through the trees, the chatter of squirrels, and the gentle rain-like sound of a neighbor's sprinklers. I watched hawks soar and swoop gracefully overhead. I heard the crows having a friendly family argument. I noticed the sky and the clouds, and I noticed the clouds when they weren't there. I felt the sun on my skin or sometimes the cool, foggy air if we were out in the morning.

---

* I read some research that suggests some birdsong in the morning may help influence the opening of plant leaves and flowers for the day. So why not humans, too? If I'm any indication, they do; their morning singing absolutely does help me start my day in a beautiful way.

A few times Luna and I came upon a deer or two foraging for something to eat, which is what happens during the dry months when the animals venture out of hiding to eat and drink and survive. They looked at me with the same measure of curiosity as I did them. "Where'd you come from?" "No, where'd *you* come from?" they seemed to reply back to me. I marveled at our presence in each other's worlds, wild animals doing their thing in the middle of a city populated by 12.5 million people.

These walks were connecting me to the world, to nature, to countless miracles, my own life included.

I would talk to myself on these perambulations through the neighborhood. No inhibitions whatsoever. I was the weird lady wearing a baseball cap and oversize sunglasses walking an aging black mutt in need of Invisalign while working out my anger and disgust for where my life currently sat. I reflected on past relationships in my life. "Really? You just let yourself be treated that way? What's wrong with you? Why did you tolerate intolerable behavior?"

"Well, you know why. Because whatever was said to you, you said worse to yourself. You were just hearing what you were already telling yourself, you ninny. It starts with you."

I kept the dialogue going. And I kept listening. And looking around me. It was as if the whole world was my therapist's office. In a way, it was therapy. I put it all out there for anyone to hear, including the sound of my thighs rubbing together, and watched those words and sounds echo through the hills until they faded into the distance, along with some of my anger. "Give it to the crows," I told myself. Luna seemed to understand.

"You know what?" I said to her one day. "I don't want to dish out blame. The onus to like myself, to treat myself lovingly, to treat others kindly and considerately, to be better, it's on me. We are all doing the best we can. I want to believe that people are innately good. And I do believe that. I really think we are. I think a lot of the trauma and pain we experience in childhood and continue to reexperience as adults covers up that natural goodness and happiness and causes us to lash out and treat each other cruelly. And sometimes—often times—the person we treat the worst is ourselves."

One day as Luna and I headed down the driveway, I was thinking about my girlfriend, having had dinner with her the night before. Several months had passed since the accident, and she had traded her walker for a cane. I was so proud of how she had walked through the restaurant to our table and told her so.

"Baby steps," she said. "Soon I'll be dancing."

With a smile on my face and Luna by my side, I realized how nice it was to leave the house without a destination. I never asked myself where I was going or which direction I was taking, or where I was supposed to get to. It was nice to walk, just to walk, with myself, with God, with the universe, with joy, with a crappy attitude, with a problem, and without knowing or caring whether I was going to turn right or left. Whatever was going on, no matter how I felt, I would step out of the noise and work through whatever it was that was on my mind, until I had solved the problem or unraveled the mystery, or maybe come up with an answer that had eluded me, or counted my blessings, or just concluded that things would be okay because sometimes some things are unfixable and you find peace with that. Here's the cool thing I discovered: The road always led me to wherever I was supposed to be.

And that's why I am still walking—continually amazed at how going nowhere can take me everywhere.

my roots are showing

*"Life is not a problem to be solved,
but a reality to be experienced."*
—ATTRIBUTED TO SØREN KIERKEGAARD

JOURNAL ENTRY, OCTOBER 2022

EVERY FEW WEEKS I catch myself in the bathroom mirror. Not to admire or assess—at least not consciously—but because something feels slightly off. It's morning, the sun still on the rise. I wake up early, and my head is still filled with enough sleepy fog that I need a few minutes before I can see clearly. I splash water on my face, peer into the glass, and then I see it: My roots are showing.

And so begins the debate—should I or shouldn't I color my roots? I know this might seem trite, a mere blip on the list of things that matter in life, ranking somewhere around dealing with people who constantly apologize for things that don't require an apology. "You don't have to say you're sorry." "Okay, sorry." I've had that exact conversation with people. And I should probably apologize for sharing this should-I-or-shouldn't-I dialogue I have with myself about coloring my roots.

It's the molehill that I've turned into a mountain, my monthly version of the movie *Tootsie*. Whether to color my hair, though, is only the surface issue. Am I covering up my true identity? Maybe the real question—the one lurking in the shadows—is about something else. Who do I see when I look at myself? Who am I looking at? There's the version the world sees and the me that only I know. The inside me and the outside me. Is one more important than the other? Should they sync up? What if they don't?

I've lived this quandary practically my entire life, this morning *knock-knock-who's-there*. There was getting monthly zits and seeing my body develop and change, the blush of being in love, marveling at my round belly as a life grew inside it, hating my puffy eyes from crying while going through a divorce, wishing I was five or ten pounds lighter and my hips were slimmer, and so on. I've stared at all of it, trying to reconcile what I saw with how I felt. And now, in my sixties, there's this matter of my roots.

It starts innocently. My first reaction is a shrug. "Eh, no one will notice." A few days later, I say to myself, "Girl, you have to make an appointment." After another few days of procrastination, I make sure to leave a baseball cap next to my bed to grab if there's an earthquake in the middle of the night and I have to run out of the house. I don't mind if my neighbors see me in an old T-shirt and underwear, but God forbid they see my roots are showing.

Others might have a different conversation in front of their mirror. Pants versus a skirt. Makeup versus going makeup-free. Why should something so trivial matter? Because for me, it isn't really about hair. It's about self-perception and the friction between how we feel and how we appear. It's about the version of ourselves we feel comfortable showing. It's about how much of ourselves we choose to see in the mirror. We don't call it our reflection for nothing! What are we reflecting upon? What is reflecting back to us?

Gray roots are the attention-getter, the flag waving in the mirror: "Hey, are you okay with this?"

I've been asking some version of that question since I was nineteen and first started going gray. I went from *One Day at a Time* to "one gray at a time." I was still a teenager! My friends were asking where to buy pot and where to get birth control, not where to get their hair colored. I ignored the first few dozen strands, the early arrivals, as I recall them. They were like guests who show up to your party a half an hour early. You're still in your bathrobe, your hair not yet dry. The appetizers aren't ready. But you say it is fine that they've arrived early, not a problem, you're basically ready, you're just going to throw on some clothes.

"Yell to me when you hear the oven timer go off."

My timer went off on a movie set. A cinematographer lit me for a shot and suddenly called out, "You have a gray hair." He said it loud enough for everyone to hear. His assistant. The makeup artist. The director. Everyone else nearby. So much for anonymity and vanity. He plucked it out before I could protest, before I had a chance to ask God why this very noticeable part of my appearance, and my identity, was not only aging prematurely but now a topic for public conversation.

"There, it's gone," he said.

I winced. "But I liked my gray hair."

"No, no, no, you don't want that on camera."

I had no choice but to take his word. I was too busy and too young to know what I wanted on or off camera. My relationship with a prominent filmmaker was winding down. I would soon meet my future husband. I was working steadily. I was on the cover of magazines. It was the best and the worst of Hollywood. The best for obvious reasons. The worst because I would read those same magazines and compare myself with icons like Farrah, Jaclyn, Victoria, and other really, truly beautiful women and never see the flawless beauty I desperately wanted to see in myself.

Of course, I never saw what those women saw when they looked at themselves—and the truth is, they probably saw imperfections when they looked at themselves on TV or magazine covers. All of us see something no one else sees. The confusion, if not the struggle, is what we are looking for—and where we are looking. Inside or outside? Do we see the whole picture? Or only parts? What if we didn't look at all? What if all we knew was the way others saw us?

If only it were possible to time travel. I'd go back and meet the good person of Anatolia (now present-day Turkey) who first polished obsidian around 6000 BCE and ask why they felt the need to check themselves out, thereby dooming all of us who came after to a lifetime of reflecting on an image that doesn't show the entirety of who we really are as human beings dealing with the simple fact of existing.

* * *

The same cinematographer was not finished with me. Later in the production, after he lit another shot, he examined me again and shook his head. He spotted something on the side of my nose, touched it with his finger, and summoned the makeup artist. I wondered what was going on.

"We're going to do something about your bump," he said.

"What bump?" I asked.

He put his finger on the side of my nose. "Right there."

"What? I've never noticed a bump."

He shrugged. "It's uneven."

I was stunned. I'd always loved my nose. I thought it was a cute little button nose. Apparently one side had a little bump that was higher than the other side. I had done 209 episodes of *One Day at a Time* without anyone saying a word about it. Why was it a problem now? Did this cinematographer want it to look like someone else's nose? Or just a better, more symmetrical nose? Why did he immediately assume that I didn't want a nose bump, either?

What if that unevenness was something that made me unique? I suppose it's not a what-if question. It was one of the many pieces that added up to make me, well, me—and here this guy wanted to "do something about" it, to smooth it out. Who are we supposed to be if not ourselves? What's the point of hiding our bumps? It took years for me to understand the importance of these questions.

When I was in junior high, my father compared my figure—or lack of one—to my older cousin's; she was shaped more like an hourglass than a ruler. I also had a teacher who rested his hand on my soft stomach and warned, not unkindly but with an authoritative tone, that I should "watch it." I wish I had asked why—why did I have to watch it? I was being trained from a young, fragile, impressionable age to look at what was apparently wrong with me, to equate flaws with failure, and to identify the parts of myself that didn't measure up to some standard of perfection.

That kind of scrutiny isn't just something you limit to yourself. It infects how you see everyone else. You start measuring. Comparing. Are they prettier? Smarter? Thinner? Do their thighs touch when they walk? You stop seeing people as whole. You see only what you believe they have that you don't. In art, that emptiness is called negative space. In real life, it's a space of insecurity and self-loathing.

My friends and I spent hours with magazines open in front of us. We wanted Christie's nose, Cindy's legs, Farrah's hair. The magazines urged us to pay attention to what was "Red Hot Now" and "The Best of the Best." Each month had its "new dazzle" and beauty breakthroughs. We were told to Jazzercise, dance to the oldies, go on a protein-only diet, or stick to just cabbage soup. Would we ever achieve that kind of beauty? Of course not. Not when there's a new issue, with new tips, every month.

I didn't mind being a work in progress. Hell, I'm still a work in progress. The problem was, and probably always will be, that rarely do we see the full picture—not in ourselves, and not in others. That's the danger of mirrors. They only show the surface. And even then, only from one angle.

* * *

My best angle was one the cinematographer never saw. Because it was impossible to see. It had nothing to do with the way I looked, nothing that showed up in his camera. It was the way I felt inside. I remember feeling it twice. The first was with Ed, in the precious days when our relationship was new and still simple and innocent. We were madly in love and starting out.

I was in my early twenties, wide-eyed and dreaming of a future full of possibilities, and Ed, though slightly older, was similar. We would have conversations deep into the night about ourselves, about our fears and hopes, about life. They were raw and intimate and real. I never once talked about how I wanted to look. Only about how I wanted to feel—and what I felt was a sense of lightness.

I felt the same way when I was pregnant with my son, Wolfie. My stomach grew. I gained weight. I woke up every day thinking only about how I felt, how the baby felt, how freaking exciting it was to become a mother. I gained sixty-plus pounds. I loved the way I looked. I never once felt heavy or fat, only a sense of lightness and joy.

I still feel that way about my relationship with my son even though he's in his thirties, married, and quite independent. Ed and I also ended up light. At the last Thanksgiving we shared, he took me outside and opened his heart in a way he said was way past due. We both did. We found a place of deep love and forgiveness for our past mistakes. My final words to him when he was taking his last breaths in the hospital were "I love you." I'm so grateful to have had that sense of lightness.

This is what I look for now in the mirror. I know if I feel that way inside, that sense of lightness, the outside will be just fine.

* * *

In my early twenties I put streaks in my hair. I wanted to play with it. It was the '80s. Hair was big, and mine was huge. It was also feathered. Sometimes I put caramel streaks in it; other times blond streaks. I was having fun. The occasional gray strand was ignored or greeted with a friendly "Oh, hello" and quickly forgotten. I was married, and life as a twentysomething actress and rock star wife was loose and busy.

Then one day I was doing a photo shoot for the cover of *Us* magazine. I was twenty-eight, and my hair was pulled back, no bangs. The photographer handed me a couple of Polaroid test shots. I held up one for everyone to see. "Look at my gray hair," I said proudly.

I loved it. I always looked so much younger than I was, but finally I was starting to look grown up, mature. It was the kind of reaction you have when you see everything that's right about yourself. The so-called imperfections are considered and embraced, adding to the uniqueness of your luster, the glow that starts on the inside and radiates outward, the calm that helps to weather the storms, the inner tapestry of hard-earned equanimity that is exposed through life experience.

I pointed it out to friends. "They're signs of wisdom," one said. "A beautiful shot," another said. "I don't see any gray," another added, lying, obviously.

Then the gray began to take over. It turned out the early arrivals were saving seats for their friends. Soon they were having a block party on my head. I started coloring my hair. I stopped while I was pregnant with Wolfie, but I started again after he was born. I thought I was too young to go gray. Every two to three weeks I got my hair colored. In the '80s and '90s, going to the salon was like being at a party. I spent two or three hours there, listening to who was sleeping with whom, who was doing what drugs, and which restaurants and clubs everyone was going to (we very rarely did that and so I lived vicariously), all while great music played in the background. A glass of champagne? Yes, please.

All through the '90s, I played with different shades and tones from brown to black to blond. I permed my hair, put extensions in, and cut it short. I feathered my bangs, then did away with them altogether. I was growing up, driving carpools, and spending Saturdays at the soccer or T-ball field. Marriage had its rocky moments, but whose didn't? At the salon, the talk was about who was working, who was having work done, whose marriage was over, who was cheating, and who was in rehab. The champagne went away. Just herbal tea, thanks.

In her classic book *I Feel Bad About My Neck*, one of my favorites, the brilliant and hilarious screenwriter Nora Ephron wrote that hair dye was the only surefire way to combat aging. She had a point, which she supported by noting that she did not know one woman her age with gray hair. For the most part, I have to concur. But I also think hair dye, along with cosmopolitans, antidepressants, and spiritual retreats, is a preferred method for dealing with emotional crises. Your husband is cheating? Go blond. Getting a divorce? Go blond. Turning fifty? Cut it off and go blond.

I was blond in 2018, drank Cosmos, and booked a long weekend at a spiritual retreat. Don't ask.

* * *

A year later, I tried Botox. I didn't like it and had a mini freak-out when I saw it changed the shape of my eyebrows, which changed the shape of my face, which was a shock because my face is the way I recognize myself. I didn't like what I saw. I didn't want to see a puffy, distorted version of me in the mirror. I didn't want to wake up and say, "Knock knock, is Val there?"

During lockdown, everything changed. I couldn't go to the salon, and frankly, I didn't need to. I wasn't seeing anyone except Wolfie and his then-girlfriend-future-wife, Andraia. They would visit the cats, have dinner with me, and curl up on the sofa for weekly Marvel movie nights.* I wasn't working. I wasn't leaving the house. I wasn't being seen.

So, I let my hair grow. The gray roots didn't just show—they took over. And slowly, something else surfaced. A sense of calm. Equanimity. I looked in the mirror and didn't flinch. I didn't ask

---

* We went through the entire series chronologically. So fun!

if I looked good. I asked how I felt. It was a new question—and a better one.

I listened to music that helped me feel strong—Aretha, Taylor Swift, Kelly Clarkson, P!nk. I did puzzles. I walked. I grieved Ed. I grieved the loss of my parents. I came to terms with the end of my second marriage. I cooked. And every time I saw my reflection in the mirror or a window or a Zoom on my computer screen, I thought, "Okay. This is who you are. This is how you look. And this is how you feel. And you're okay."

I looked into my eyes. I smiled. Once, maybe twice, I even winked. Who gives themselves a wink? I guess I do. Try it. If you're anything like me, it will make you giggle.

That feeling—the one I used to call lightness—came back, faintly, quietly, but with a slight melancholy to it, like a memory you don't expect to return. It was how I felt in the early days with Ed, talking deep into the night, vulnerable and open, no performance, no persona. That version of us didn't last, of course. We both lost our way, buried under ambition, addiction, fear. But we had that moment. That realness. And we had it again, a peaceful grace, in the year leading up to his death.

I feel fortunate that it returned.

So maybe it's not about what we look like or who we look like, but whether we see a good, thoughtful, giving person when we look in the mirror. Even simpler: Do we see a person rather than a figure? Do we reflect on who we are to each other? Who we are to ourselves? Do we look at our behavior more than our body? Do we tend to our wounds more than our wrinkles? Do we understand that the essence of who we are, our real beauty, has nothing to do with hairstyles or dress sizes but something else deep inside us, the way we draw a breath, the way we smile, the way we cry through pain, through joy, the way we offer help to those who need it, the way we tend our spirit, the way we find peace and understanding in our humanity?

I know that's a lot to see, daunting in fact, like trying to find a parking space at Trader Joe's, but it's all present in the mirror, within us, waiting to be seen.

After lockdown ended, my manager called. "You have to shoot your book cover. You have to look like Valerie."

Who's that? The little girl with brown eyes and matching hair? The teen grappling with insecurity and shame? The woman with gray roots and soft lines around her eyes? The woman in her sixties who asks not "How do I look?" but "How do I feel?"

I see so many women who look absolutely stunning when they let their gray grow out. For me, I wasn't ready. Not yet. And it wasn't about vanity. It was about reconciling who I see in the mirror with the little girl still alive inside me. She wasn't ready, either. She needed to be seen—really seen—for the first time. Not corrected. Not improved. Understood.

She was there, as were all the other versions of me. But she was special. I had to look harder, deeper, and braver to find her. I had to see behind the doors I'd locked and the shadows I'd avoided, and then I would finally see myself as I'd always wanted to be seen.

Hair dye, in case you aren't familiar, comes in different grades of color. Number 1 is pitch black and number 12 is platinum blond. Though I identified with someone who had gray hair, I wasn't ready to identify with the gray hair itself, not yet. I went with a 5/6 brown.

It looked right, like me. Even better, it felt the way I wanted to feel—light. One day I'll let it grow out and go gray. I'm curious what that will feel like.

But for now, I need to match the outside with the inside, and I'm still finding the line between them. I'm still finding that little girl.

puzzles

Self-compassion, mindfulness
Recognizing this is part of the human condition.
Self-kindness

JOURNAL ENTRY, AUGUST 2022

IN MY TV room, along the wall that leads from the kitchen to the staircase going up to my office, I have created a gallery of family photographs. The wall is long—perfect for generations of Italians, Dutch, English, Indonesians, and Irish—in other words, a large family. And for me, "family" is not just those who are part of my bloodline. It reaches beyond to include the family I was born into, gave birth to, married into, and those who are instrumental in my life.

I've been working on this project for two years. It's therapy. It's a puzzle. Luckily for me, I love puzzles.

This is not my first rodeo with a gallery wall. I have curated several of these over many years. They change as I change. I put together one during my last marriage. When that ended, I took it down and repainted the wall. I wanted a fresh start. I feel like I start fresh a lot, more than most people perhaps. I'm always starting over without ever quite filling all the frames in my gallery, like a puzzle that's missing a piece or two or three. Maybe that's the point.

There are thirty-one picture frames on my wall right now. Six are empty—I can't explain why except that I haven't found the right pictures. Maybe they're the pieces I haven't figured out yet. Maybe they're placeholders for . . . I don't know, grandchildren perhaps? Fingers are crossed. But hey, no pressure. I have a few photos from early in Wolfie and Andraia's relationship—they're adorable—and one from their perfect wedding celebration in October 2023. There are also a couple of shots of Wolfie and his dad and several of my son that I took when he was a child—in our backyard, at school, throwing a snowball in Park City, and one of him about an hour after he was born, cradled in Ed's brother Al's hand.

I love that picture. It's been more than thirty-four years since then, and still, every time I look at that picture, I stop and marvel and think, "My body did that."

At the other end of the wall is a gorgeous portrait that noted photographer Mark Seliger took of Ed, me, and Wolfie for *Rolling Stone* magazine. Ed and I had been having troubles here and there, but we were going through a calm and loving spell at the time, and I can look at myself in that picture and see that I was appreciating it. Near that one is a triptych of me, Wolfie, and Ed—each at eighteen months old—where the three of us look identical. That resemblance still boggles my mind.

In fact, the whole thing all kind of blows me away. From the picture of Wolfie on his way to the Grammys for his first nomination to the photos of my brothers and their wives. There's also a picture of my now former sister-in-law, her two boys, and her husband, whom I adore. My grandparents are up there, in sepia photos that must be close to a hundred years old. I often pause to stare at them and wonder what they were thinking and feeling when those pictures were taken.

Some of these photographs have been in the same frames for years. Each time I redo one of these gallery walls, I move them around and blend them with the new pictures. It's an ever-expanding, changing, complicated tapestry of family, of life being lived. All the different-size frames, the chaos—I'm always shifting, moving, and reframing photos, similar to the way I'm always trying to figure out the puzzle that's me, and somehow they all go together. Don't ask me how, but somehow they do.

* * *

Decades ago my brother Drew gifted me with a puzzle table. He built it himself; that's the kind of handy guy he is. It was like a medium-size coffee table, but with shelves underneath for storing more puzzles and small lips on the top to keep puzzle pieces from falling off. I thought that was clever.

I always had a puzzle going over the holidays and during family visits. It might take a long, sleepless weekend to finish one of those thousand piecers, and you don't want to lose any pieces. Still, occasionally, I'd get close to finishing and discover that one was missing. I'd immediately get up to see if I was sitting on it. I'd check under the sofa cushions. I'd ask the cats if one of them ate it.

If it was still missing after a thorough investigation, I doubled down on my feline housemates like I was Mariska Hargitay from *Law & Order*. "Did one of you take it? Tell me the truth now and I'll put in a good word with the DA." But no one ever admitted to taking the missing piece, and I believed them. So where did it go? Another puzzle to solve!

This is my life in a sense, solving puzzles. I have my jigsaws. I'm also addicted to my daily crossword. That's the main reason (well, that and the food section) I still get an old-fashioned print edition of the *Los Angeles Times* delivered to the end of my driveway every morning, the way it was back in the olden days. Then there is Wordle (I did it in three today) and Connections, which drives me crazy when I can't get it. I'll reach a point where I press all the keys on my phone, turn it off, and get on with my day.

Hours later I will chastise myself for losing patience: "You could've figured it out if you'd just taken a little more time." That's one of the things about puzzles. They teach patience, focus, and persistence. They remind us that things don't always come easily, not without trial and error. They require us to think about how the pieces fit together. Puzzles take time.

Both of my parents have passed away, but before they did, we moved them from their home in Peoria, Arizona, to an assisted living facility. During that transition, my brothers and I went through the ritual common to people our age of cleaning out our parents' house and garage. I brought home most of the family photo albums my dad had put together over the years. I didn't open some of them for a long time. I'm talking a couple of years. I wasn't that curious, and too many things were going on.

Then one day I randomly pulled one off the shelf and flipped it open. There was a photo of me and my brother David playing in front of a yellow convertible parked on a small hill—the hill we would sled on in the winter. Later that day, David and I snuck into that car and one of us released the emergency brake. The car rolled down the hill and hit the neighbor's car.

We were scared to death. We knew we were in trouble. My dad worked for General Motors, and he brought home a different car every few weeks to test-drive. This was one of those cars. David and I got out of the car and ran directly to our rooms. As my mom called everyone for dinner, there was a knock on the front door. It was the police. You can imagine our parents' surprise.

The police took an accident report. David and I thought we were going to jail. I wasn't even eight years old and I thought I was going to spend the rest of my life behind bars. Our parents were livid, but we didn't end up in the slammer, just grounded for a week, which was, thankfully, far more appropriate.

I flipped a few pages further in the album and found a picture of myself wearing a beautiful blue double-breasted mini coat with a white collar that my mom had made me for Easter. We had just come home from church. I had on my white tights, white shoes, a white hat with a blue band, a little white purse, and my precious coat. The kids across the street were playing baseball.

"Go in and take that jacket off and put on your play clothes," my mom said. "I don't want you going over there and getting dirty."

I can still hear myself saying, "Fine, fine."

But rather than change, I crossed the street to watch the kids playing baseball. Suddenly, a ball came straight at me. I froze and got hit in the middle of my face. I ended up with two black eyes and a bloody nose that dripped all over my beautiful coat. My mom was so upset, but not as upset as I was about ruining that coat. I cried and cried. Lesson learned.

Then I saw a picture of me and my cousin Elaine after our first Holy Communion. Another one of us taking my grandmother to see the nuns at the cloister near where they lived in Chester County, Pennsylvania, which she liked to do on weekends. I sat next to her on these drives and remember the way she gently tapped her fingers to the music playing in the car. She had beautiful hands. I was always mesmerized by the skill and dexterity of those hands as she kneaded dough for bread and shaped fresh cappelletti and gnocchi.

I flipped the page to another picture of my parents on a ski trip—the one when my mom broke her leg. A later photo showed her in bed, with a full leg cast, and me and two of my brothers sitting with her.

Inside a different album I found a picture of myself as a little girl holding a cat. I looked at a few more pages. Almost all the photos of me in this section showed me holding a cat—not all of them the same. I remembered some of those cats with immediate clarity. I could feel their fur. Others I had zero recollection of. None whatsoever, which bothered me.

I sat on the floor with several more albums. My dad had done an excellent job organizing and curating these family photos. But I saw myself in more photos of which I had no memory. I was startled by how much of my childhood I couldn't remember. There it was in front of me, and I had no recollection. I've always prided myself on having an excellent memory. I've spent most of my life memorizing lines for work. Fifty or sixty pages of dialogue. I've never shown up on a TV or movie set unprepared.

My childhood was similar. I could picture every place we had lived, from Delaware to Michigan to Los Angeles to Shreveport, Louisiana. Our homes, riding my bicycle, meals at my aunt's house, family vacations. Yet some of these photo albums left me clueless. Chunks of my life were missing. Where did those pieces go?

* * *

When I was growing up, we were a happy family. At least that was the narrative my parents told us, especially my father. He always made it clear to us kids that we had a good life. I can still hear him underscore that fact from the front seat of the family station wagon: "So be grateful for it."

I was grateful, without questioning it. I had a fortunate childhood compared with those of so many others, like my friend and former

One Day at a Time costar Mackenzie Phillips. My family was stable. My dad's job at GM was a good one, and he rose up the ranks, and my mother was a devoted stay-at-home mom. She was a gifted painter. Always exhausted and underappreciated. We visited relatives and took family vacations. My parents entertained. Everyone loved my dad, and they loved my mother's party platters even more.

Beneath the veneer of that good life, though, was a layer of darkness. Both of my parents had rough upbringings. They had a child who died at seventeen months. There were infidelities on my father's part. My mother suffered silently, crying on occasion but never to my knowledge fighting back. They soldiered through their issues. We all did. We had a good life. We really did. *Be grateful for it.*

I think I am a grateful person. I have my share of "why me" moments, but I constantly remind myself how much I have to be grateful for. I love my son and his wife and the fact he has found his person. I love my brothers, their wives, my girlfriends, their husbands and children, my career, my home, my beautiful garden, and all my cats and my dog, Luna. I love that I am healthy. I love my connection with fans. I love both of my coffee machines. I love my zester. I could go on. I'm blessed. I overflow with gratitude.

But . . .

I hate that there's a but, but there is. It's because I'm the child of parents who kept secrets from us and each other. They hid the dishonesty in their relationship. I didn't know the details, but like many children, I sensed it, and speaking as a twice-married, twice-divorced woman, that's affected my own relationships. I'm wary of intimacy and unable to trust. Or I'm too trusting and hold on too long. I've been in love. I think I might want to fall in love again. But . . .

This puzzle is a hard one.

* * *

The chilly months of 2024 and early 2025 were hard. I walked around asking myself where my empathy went. It disappeared on me, like a sweater I couldn't find. Where did I put it? A lot of people I knew were grumpy or out of sorts. The world was in flux. Too much was happening. The conversations we must have, mostly with ourselves, to understand our connection to each other were lost in the loud clamor of division. So much anger was in the air. It was easy to feel overwhelmed and tune out, and I mostly did. But the numbness—or was it indifference?—bothered me. It wasn't me. Something was amiss.

In the past I would've ignored this and gone about my business, perhaps a little like my parents had done for most of their marriage, letting the layers of frustrations, irritations, grief, distrust, and whatever else they felt pile up, a thickening of the skin, a purposeful obliviousness. Except I was trying to avoid that callousness. I didn't want to live this way.

It was not a comfortable place to be. It was not a pleasant way to feel. Change started on the freeway, of all places. I was in traffic, waiting to exit the 101 at the Laurel Canyon off-ramp. I could've walked faster than the cars were moving. As I inched closer to the exit, someone wedged their way in front of the car ahead of me, ignoring the zipper method of traffic merging. "Don't let him in," I shouted. "Don't let him in." Then: "Son of a . . ."

What kind of person decides they don't have to wait like everyone else? Who cuts in line like that? Where have the little acts of decency that hold all of us together gone? Opening a door for someone? Waiting your turn at a four-way stop? Talking to your neighbors? Sending a thank-you note? Simple tolerance for each other no matter our beliefs or differences? Trust and predictability are how we get along in this great big, crowded, complicated world. We learn this in elementary school. Wait your turn. No cuts! Follow the rules. As adults, we commit to the common good. Then some jerk pushes their way in front of the line and ruins it for everyone else. I was livid.

Then a thought came to me. What if they had a good reason for cutting that I didn't know about? I mean, how could I know? That driver could have been a selfish jerk or he might've been sick. He might've had an emergency situation. Maybe his kid got hurt at school. Maybe he had to go to the bathroom really bad. There were missing pieces to this puzzle. I didn't know the entire story. Do we ever know it?

It wasn't like I hadn't had similar thoughts before. How many times had I looked at someone on a plane, in a store, at a restaurant, or in the checkout line at the grocery store and wondered, "What's their story?" As an actress, I've always been interested in people's stories. Intrigued by the doors that would let me step into character—what's obvious, what's unseen? But stuck in traffic, my thoughts were more personal than professional, about how everyone is going through something, and more than likely, multiple things—aches and pains, parents, kids, job, worries about life . . . something.

I did several seasons of *Valerie's Home Cooking* while my marriage was falling apart. No one knew. Though I can watch and see when chopping onions wasn't the only reason I had tears in my eyes. I remembered being on movie sets years earlier when I would've preferred to be driving Wolfie's carpool. God, I can still feel the ache from missing my kid. Or waiting impatiently at CVS when my mom was sick, thinking, "Come on, people. Let's go," all the while smiling lest someone go home and say, "I saw Valerie Bertinelli. What a bitch."

We're all jugglers, trying and hoping not to drop a ball—especially in public. But it happens, you know—and then you're the jerk on the freeway who cuts someone off. Or you're the individual giving that person the middle finger without thinking that something else might be going on. We must keep this in mind. We must remind ourselves to consider each other the way that we want others to consider us. We're all neighbors on this planet.

I was still thinking about this when I got home and noticed that one of my cats—I'm not mentioning any names, Nelson—had peed in the kitchen sink. Why? He had never done that before. What was going on with him? What message was he trying to send me?*

This is the root of empathy—knowing there is probably more to the story, trying to figure out what that is, and understanding that in some way I am part of it, too.

* * *

Back on my gallery wall, the pictures from the family photo albums began to speak to me. One of my mom as a young woman caught my eye. I was standing next to her. My brothers too. We were little. My mom had all her kids before she was twenty-seven. She was beautiful. I always thought she was gorgeous, but as I studied the photograph, her looks impressed me in a new way. Her youth was still visible. Her smile was my smile.

I got emotional looking at her. I had spent so much of my life trying to find myself, trying to prove I was different from my mom,

---

* A few days later, he had trouble breathing. It turned out Nelson had issues with his kidney and heart. He was, in that special way animals have, sending me a message. It was the beginning of the end.

only to realize in my mid-sixties that I am more like her than I wanted to admit. She was someone who kept her feelings inside. Who put everyone else's happiness before her own. Who didn't complain. Who smiled through hard times. As a kid I took that for granted, if I even noticed, but now I realized the incredible inner strength that required. She was a survivor. Her mother died when she was nine. Her father remarried, and she hated her stepmother, whom she always described as cruel. My mom was barely seventeen when she got pregnant; she married my dad four months later. I think she just wanted to get the hell out of that house.

It worked. My dad fell in love with a beautiful girl, and it was the '50s, you know; you got married at seventeen and twenty years old. Of course, who am I to talk? I was only twenty when I married Ed. My dad had crazy-high expectations for people, including himself. He knew everybody's name. And everybody liked Andy. He worked hard to provide for his family, though one consequence of that was we moved around a lot for his work. By the time I was a teenager, we had lived in five different states.

Fitting in and making friends in school, a challenge in any child's life, was a nerve-racking norm for me through high school. "Just be nice. People will like you," my dad said. While that is good, practical advice, it doesn't reflect much sensitivity to the insecurity I had when starting my third new school in six years. But that was my dad, focused on likability and looks.

He was loving but judgmental to me, and stern and truculent with my brothers. With my mom, he was unpredictable. Loving and kind one day and critical and aloof on another. Unfaithful when we were growing up yet devoted to her during their last years together.

That was the model I saw of love and marriage. A man who vocalized his love for his wife yet scarred her emotionally with infidelity and thoughtlessness. I'm still trying to undo that tangled yarn of what intimate love is between two people.

My dad passed on December 7, 2016.

On the eighth anniversary of his death, I sat at my kitchen table and looked at photos of him in album after album. At the time, I was having several recurring dreams at night. In one, I was drowning and would wake up feeling helpless. In another, the one I had most often, I was walking through a house in which a few rooms were scary, especially on the upper floor. Each time I started to climb the stairs, I would wake up with my heart thumping against my chest.

I googled an online dream dictionary and found the obvious: These rooms represented scary places in my brain I didn't want to enter. They were the places I kept the parts of my childhood I couldn't or didn't want to remember. And what of the parts I did remember?

My eyes filled with tears. I was in my bedroom and my dad threw open the door. "Young lady, your mother said you have not cleaned this room." Before I could say anything, and before he had assessed the situation for himself, he pushed over my dresser. It fell over onto the floor with a heavy thud. The drawers came out, clothes spilled, and whatever I had on top flew off. Now there really was a mess.

Without uttering another word, he turned abruptly and walked out of the room, slamming the door behind him. His rage left me scared and shaking.

I also remembered hearing him in the garage with my brothers, screaming and getting physical. *Dad, I heard you.* His temper seemed to come out of nowhere. *Dad, this is me and you in this picture. See. Your arm is around me. I know you loved me.* I turned the page. I was holding a cat in one of the pictures. I remembered the way I used to talk to myself back then. In a whisper only I could hear: *My dad doesn't get angry a lot. It's scary when he does, but it's not that often, so I guess it's okay.*

My dad's father, Nazzareno Bertinelli, left a wife and young son in Italy, moved to America, worked in the coal mines, and married my grandmother Angelina. I still don't know whether Nonnie knew that her husband had another family in Italy, and given the Bertinellis' poor communication skills, I doubt she did. My father eventually knew—not that he told us.

However, after he died, we found a couple of letters from his half brother among the papers he saved, referencing our grandfather's two marriages. We were shocked, totally gobsmacked. *Whoa, Grandpa had two families? Were we the A family or the B family? He lived here, with us, so that must mean something.* We were joking, but we wished my dad were still with us so we could basically ask, WTF? When did Dad find out? How did he find out? What did he think? Did it shatter his sense of family? Did it rock his world in some other way?* Did Mom know?

That raised another question: What did Mom know about Dad? And if she knew, how much did she know?

* * *

I suspect she knew everything, and through an almost incomprehensible exercise of strength, self-loathing, emotional masochism, and plain old survival instinct, she kept it to herself. I didn't realize this

---

* My life was rocked when I found out my dad was fooling around on my mom. I'm sure my mom's was, too. We knew. We didn't talk about any of it.

when I was coming of age. When I was on *One Day at a Time*, my dad had a girlfriend whom he wanted me to hire as my assistant. Though I didn't know she was his girlfriend at the time, I suspected something wasn't right. Why did he care who I hired? Why did I need to hire anyone? And why her? Kids pick up on these things.

"I'm not going to hire Vickie," I told him. "I don't want an assistant. I don't need an assistant. I'm a teenager."

I was pissed at him in general, and more specifically for putting me in that situation, and rather than hold him accountable, I transferred all my anger onto my mom. *Why didn't she say something about Vickie? What didn't she do that made my dad want to have this woman around?* Back then, at least in the environment in which I was being raised, it was the woman's responsibility to keep the man happy. In our house, that meant keeping my father and my three brothers happy.

I saw the pleading in my mom's expressions: "Don't rock the boat. This is the way things are." It's such BS now, and I suppose I knew it was back then, too. Magazines featured stories about women's rights. Men were referred to as male chauvinist pigs. A cigarette commercial on TV included a catchy song with the lyrics, "You've come a long way, baby, to get where you've got to today." If we'd come such a long way, how come we had to be so passive and subservient?

I was terrible to my mom. I got mad at her for no reason. As I went through puberty, I made her the recipient of all my anger, confusion, and frustration, which probably meant I felt safest with her without realizing it. But I knew very little about her and understood her less.

She was still a young woman carrying around an unimaginable amount of grief, which I also didn't understand. Grief for marrying a man because she was pregnant. Grief for the man who didn't love her the way she needed and deserved to be loved. And grief for the loss of her second-born, my brother Mark, before he turned two. My mom never talked about him. We didn't even find out about him until we were teenagers.

My brother Patrick first learned about Mark when he opened the linen closet and pulled out a blanket. My mom happened to be walking by and freaked out. "Don't touch that blanket!" she said. "That was Mark's blanket." Patrick let go of it and gave my mom a look like she had lost her mind and was seeing ghosts. We had no idea till then, but she was seeing a ghost—our baby brother, Mark.

Talk about a missing puzzle piece!

It wasn't until I was pregnant with Wolfie that my mom started to open up about Mark. Before then, details about him came out in dribs and drabs. But once I was carrying my own child, she told me about her own pregnancy and what Mark had been like as a baby and a toddler. He was her second boy, a bright light, happy and adventurous. He wandered off one afternoon and drank from a glass Coke bottle sitting on a barn shelf without knowing it was storing poison. A part of my mom died that day, too.

Toward the end of my pregnancy, my mom asked me to name the baby Mark if it was a boy. Ed and I didn't want to know the baby's sex ahead of time, and we hadn't yet picked out a name.* My mom made her suggestion as casually as she could. By this time, I recognized the significance of it and tried to be as sensitive as I could to her. But I explained that I wanted to pick out a name that Ed and

---

* Ed and I discussed a few names for a girl but never decided on one. We were similarly undecided on a boy's name. Then one night we popped a video of the movie *Amadeus* in our VCR, and I loved the way actress Elizabeth Berridge said the name Wolfie in the scene where she is searching for Mozart, who is hiding from her. "Wolfie! Wolfie!" she says. I turned to Ed and said, "What a great name!" And so it was.

I both liked. Truth be told, I didn't want to name my baby after my dead brother.

Did that make me a terrible person? An insensitive daughter? I didn't think so, and I still don't. I also think my mother understood. In hindsight, so much more was being said in that simple request than was actually spoken. My mom was trying to hand me a piece of the puzzle that she realized had been missing, one that she'd been holding on to for thirty years and wanted me to see.

* * *

My parents stayed together. Their marriage, lasting more than sixty years, survived as long as they did. My mom suffered from rheumatoid arthritis, and when it got really bad, she needed to be hospitalized off and on. One time, during a bad spell, my dad was working on the English side of the Channel Tunnel project. We assumed he was having an affair because he stayed over there for long stretches of time. I took my mom to her appointments. My brothers took her when I couldn't. I hated seeing my mom that vulnerable.

At one point, my dad returned home to visit my mom and all of us kids told him that his absences were no longer appropriate. *She's your wife, you should be taking care of her*, we said. *We love her, but we're doing all the things you should be doing.* To his credit, my dad stepped up. He kept detailed, daily notes on her medications and doctor visits. His files were meticulous. We saw why he was such a great manager at GM.

I think he was coming around to feel more in love with my mom—or at least he appreciated her in a way that he should have long before.

Then one day, while he sat in the waiting room during one of my mom's appointments, the nurse at the front desk noticed he didn't look well. She had him checked out and sure enough, he was having a heart attack at that exact moment. A week later, he had open-heart surgery. Once he recovered, we moved my parents to an assisted living facility. Both needed help.

Months later, my dad was sitting in the lobby, getting ready to take the shuttle to the drugstore, when he saw a woman about to trip. He ran over to help her and she fell on top of him. He broke his hip as he fell. Two months later, he was dead. In the interim, he lost all his autonomy. Seeing him helpless like that, I had the most compassion I'd ever had for my dad.

He was someone who cared about the way he looked, the way he acted, how people saw him, and what they thought, and it was all gone. He had become what he never wanted to be—a vulnerable, injured, dependent old man. I could see he was scared. And he was so angry. Like his father had been after suffering a stroke that left him a brittle old man who just grumbled and groaned. My dad used to say to us, "No, no, he was a great man. I wish you had known him before his stroke."

My heart bled for my dad. I finally saw that he was human. I also saw that he harbored his own burdens, hurts, and secrets. After he passed away, we found confirmation of one of his affairs in a letter that was among various papers in his desk. There was no point in telling my mom. Why upset her? She died a few years later, and we never knew how much she did (or didn't) know. Our family kept secrets, then those secrets kept us until they were no longer secrets.

The truth has been like a triple-strength antibiotic ointment. Applied directly to the wounds daily, and healing. I stopped judging my parents. I began looking at them as human beings who did their best and would've done better if they'd known how. They learned (or didn't) from their parents and grandparents, as my brothers and I learned from our parents. We learned what love is. We learned how to love. And we learned we could, in our own way, do better.

Thinking about my parents after their deaths has been an interesting journey. I have such compassion for the human beings they were. Doing their best with no road map or model on how to get through it. Like all of us, life bandied them about as if they were on a great ship passing through a nor'easter. Clinging to the rails just trying to get to the eye of the storm to catch their breath. I've had a lot of conflicted feelings about how I sometimes treated them or if I had even tried to understand them while they were living.

Now that they're gone, I look at that side of me that was so judgy. It makes me cringe. I feel guilty. But I've worked through finding forgiveness for them and me. And Mom and Dad would've done the same. What's the old saying? When you know better, you do better.

Life is a puzzle without a clear final picture. The pieces are infinite. Love. Heartbreak. Acceptance. Understanding. Forgiveness. Knowing better . . . You find them when you're ready. You never know where or when they will turn up, but they do, eventually, if you keep looking, as I have. The photo gallery on my wall is proof. The previous one featured a large photo of me and my ex in the center. In the version I'm working on now, my parents are in the middle. It's a better fit. And the six empty frames? I'll fill them soon, I'm positive of that.

climate change

*I have to slow down, get out of survival mode.
I need to learn better coping mechanisms.*

JOURNAL ENTRY, JULY 2024

WARNING: I AM not going to get political here, but I am going to talk about climate change. Not the change you have heard news reports about—the one causing the damage and devastation that will occur on the planet if the temperature rises two degrees Celsius above preindustrial levels. I want to talk about my *own* more personal, intimate encounter with climate change.

I was around fifty when it hit. I was eating lunch with a reporter at the Polo Lounge inside the landmark pink-and-green Beverly Hills Hotel. The Polo Lounge is one of those lunch spots in the city known as a favorite for multiple generations of Hollywood stars and power brokers. Honestly, it is a little too fancy for me to feel comfortable. But the booths are private and a great place to have a quiet interview.

Also, the most famous entrée on the lunch menu, the McCarthy salad, is priced just under fifty dollars. It's pretty much a Cobb salad—chicken, egg, bacon, roasted beets, tomato, cheddar cheese, avocado, balsamic dressing—supposedly created in a bygone era for a millionaire regular who requested something easy to chew after breaking his jaw playing polo. The story sounds apocryphal. How is that easy to eat after a broken jaw? Anyway, the rest of us have been ponying up ever since. I mean, fifty bucks for a salad? It's delicious, but c'mon!

But I digress. We were midway through lunch when my body seemed to catch fire. It began like most conflagrations, with a small burst of heat, as if a match had been struck deep inside me. The flame caught and the fire spread until it consumed me, like heat radiating up from the asphalt on an extremely hot day. I looked around to see if anyone else was suddenly uncomfortably hot. I tugged at my blouse a few times to let in some cooler air if possible. I looked down at the pricey dish I had ordered to make sure it was not seasoned with a Carolina Reaper.

I say that in jest, but seriously, something was going on. We were eating indoors, where it was cool, but it felt like we were outside under a blazing sun in the depths of an August heat wave—except I wasn't under an unforgiving sun, it was radiating from *inside me*. I felt the temperature rise and spread. My skin was turning red, burning. I picked up the glass of ice water in front of me and touched it to my forehead, to both cheeks, to my wrists, hoping to quell the heat. Was it noticeable? I did not want to suddenly look weird in front of the journalist.

"Are you hot?" I asked.

"No, why? Are you?"

"A little, maybe, I don't know, I think I may be having my first hot flash," I said, as sweat dripped down my back and I resisted the urge to rip off my shirt and everything else I had so carefully assembled two hours earlier.

Ten minutes later, lunch was over. I tipped the valet, got in my car, and noticed the heat wave had passed. What the . . . ? Moments earlier I had felt like a slab of meat on the grill at El Pollo Loco; now I was back to normal, demure and mindful, as they say. Was I loca? At home, I jumped on the Google to figure out what had happened to me. I filled in the search bar: "I am a fifty-year-old woman. I was at lunch and all of a sudden I got very hot. Really hot. Then it passed. What was going on with me?"

* * *

I know what you're thinking. How could she not know for sure? Could she possibly be that ignorant? The answer is yes—sort of—which I think is more typical than not. Most of us don't wait around for change to strike. We go about our business, pausing only when life taps us on the shoulder or punches us in the gut. As Gilda Radner said, "If it's not one thing, it's another." My mother had a hysterectomy when I was a little girl. I have a vivid memory of seeing her in a lot of pain. I asked what was wrong. "Nothing," she said. "Mommy is all right."

I was too young to understand what she was going through, even if she had wanted to explain, and as I got older, any back-and-forth we had about her health or her emotional challenges was minimal. I began to ask questions after I gave birth to Wolfie. But I didn't really talk to my mom about losing my brother Mark until the year before she passed away.

At that point, I was spending so much time with her as she convalesced, it was almost from having talked about everything safe that we finally touched on the one topic that was always off-limits.

"It must have been horrifying," I said.

I saw tears in her eyes. She nodded. But she was so uncomfortable broaching this awful time in her life that she didn't know how to talk about it, even though I could see her wishing she could. It remained unspoken. Like so many things.

She never told me that I was going to get my period. Another thing unspoken about. Nor was that information taught in schools. Suddenly I am bleeding and scared. What's going on with me? Am I sick? Dying? It's such a common situation—at least it was then. And of course, I was and still am the type who doesn't tell people any of this stuff when I'm going through it. (I wait fifty years and write a book.) I didn't tell a soul.

I don't even remember the day I actually got my period. I do recall hiding it from my mom and others on a monthly basis. But I must have finally said something to my mom at some point because I can still hear her saying, "Oh yeah, I thought you might start soon. I noticed some drops of blood on your underwear a few months back." Her comment washed over me because—well, because we didn't talk about that stuff—but now, even though she's passed, I'm asking, "And you didn't want to tell me anything? You didn't want to say, 'Heads up, over the next couple of months you might start feeling some weird stuff. You will start bleeding, and you won't be dying! Don't get scared.'" It's that simple, and for some reason, it can be that hard.

* * *

Thankfully, these days you can't turn on a TV talk show without hearing someone discuss menopause. Michelle Obama, Naomi Watts, Brooke Shields, Oprah Winfrey, Gwyneth Paltrow. Me! My friend Drew Barrymore whipped off her jacket while interviewing Jennifer Aniston and Adam Sandler on her talk show. "I think I'm having my first hot flash," she said. I don't know who started this trend of speaking openly about this phase of a woman's life, but I'm grateful. Thank you, ladies. I think it's a public service. It's the way many of us learn and communicate. "It helps to have that information," said Jennifer Aniston, who compared the onset of hot flashes to "some alien taking over your body, and it doesn't make sense."

It didn't for a long time. In the Middle Ages, women often didn't live long enough to go through this change. During the Enlightenment, fertility and beauty were prized, so those whose eggs had dried up, whose hair turned gray, whose skin sagged, who moved a little slower, and who had strong opinions about life were mocked and labeled as *imbalanced*. Many women did whatever they could to make their youthful looks last longer. Sound familiar? That was three hundred years ago! So much for enlightenment.

By the 1800s, menopause was recognized as "the change of life," but Victorian modesty ensured any conversation about it was whispered behind chamber doors. With the discovery of estrogen in the 1920s, menopause was seen as more of a medical condition than a natural phase of a woman's biological life. Starting in the '60s, hormone therapy offered women the chance to slow or reverse the aging process. Thirty years later, those treatments were villainized and became controversial. By 2025, we had a lot to talk about.

I arrived on the set of *Hot in Cleveland* holding a portable fan and suffering thick brain fog and considerable ignorance. Thank goodness for my costars, Jane Leeves, Wendie Malick, and Betty White, incredible women who were open, honest, helpful, caring, and all dealing with the sudden extremes of personal climate change. Well, except for Betty, whose perpetual smile, quick wit, and free-flowing wisdom revealed her journey to a better place, a freedom that helped her find the joy in each day.

I know Betty sounds too good to be true, like it was an act, but she was good and true, which was her secret. She was also tough. She was the one who said, "Butterflies are like women—we may look pretty and delicate, but, baby, we can fly through a hurricane." I mean . . . *

I would be doing a scene and out of nowhere I'd feel like I had been hiking through the Mojave Desert. Sweat would pour out of me. And

---

* With all due respect to Betty, I've read that some butterflies, sensing an impending storm, prefer to take shelter. I belong to that species, though I have flown through a few hurricanes as well.

CLIMATE CHANGE

typically, television soundstages are kept at a chilly sixty-four degrees so the actors don't sweat through their makeup. Other times the brain fog would roll in and I'd forget everything, a total whiteout. Practically all my bloopers from that show can be attributed to menopause. The ladies and I did talk about this, along with the writers, many of whom were women. The show's title was a play on menopause. Yeah, we were hot, and periodically we were boiling. Lisa, the woman who did my makeup, always carried a fan with her. It never helped much because the heat came from the inside. Like a geyser at Yellowstone. The heat boiled to such an intensity that it blew, and then it was gone for a while.

The best and funniest lines I have heard about menopause are from the classic TV series *The Golden Girls*. Dorothy (Bea Arthur), talking about menopause to Blanche (Rue McClanahan), says, "What's the big deal, Blanche? It's nothing. Look at it this way: You don't get cramps once a month. You don't go on eating binges once a month. You don't get crazy once a month."

Then Sophia (Estelle Getty) says, "You just grow a beard."

"Don't listen to her," Dorothy says.

Sophia differs. "You grow a beard, Dorothy. I woke up one morning, I looked like Arafat!"

The takeaway: Make sure you own tweezers.

* * *

I was fortunate to not go through anything more severe than a walking microclimate and waking up in a soaking-wet nightgown or T-shirt. I seem to have gotten off easy. I have friends who got zapped with very severe symptoms, from joint pain and heart issues to incontinence* and depression. At some point I wanted relief from the heat and the fog. A friend recommended a doctor who was supposed to be really good with natural remedies and other woo-woo stuff. I went to him for a while. Each visit he rubbed some ointment on my arm.

"They did this two hundred years ago," he said.

What they didn't do two hundred years ago was take MasterCard. All the treatment did was turn my menses dark brown. My hot flashes continued.

I gave up on that, and since my symptoms weren't debilitating, I told myself to buck up, that women have been getting through this since Eve first woke up in the middle of the night and threw the covers off Adam—and I bet she was sleeping in some ratty old animal-skin T-shirt. The martyr in me said I could get through it. I just had to be strong, patient, and remember to leave the window open at night.

I saw an eventual upside to this so-called change of life. In my youth, I hated bleeding every month, constantly processing eggs and sloughing them off, then going through the entire cycle again and again and again. Every month, I could feel when my egg dropped. I could feel which side it was on. It was always painful. I knew I wasn't having any more children, so for me, I felt a budding freedom. This was part of a cycle, but a new, different cycle.

The timing was interesting. I was approaching my sixties, heading toward divorce, my son was grown and embarking on his own career, and I loved my job. My body was telling me something, something important, which leads me to another whole topic: How well do we listen to our bodies? I have spent most of my life in a conversation

---

* I mean, technically, once in a while, if I laughed a bit too hard, a little pee might say "Hey," so I guess I can't really count that out.

with my body, yet I have only, for the most part, done all the talking and very little listening.

The exception was when I was pregnant and experiencing a new life growing inside me. For forty-two glorious weeks, I shut up and listened. I heard a heartbeat inside me. I heard the growing echo of hope and love. I heard the sound of a miracle.

With menopause, my body screamed, "For God's sake, open a window, woman! Stand by the air-conditioning. Take off your clothes. I'm on fire!" I couldn't help but hear what it was saying. During my twenties, some people thought I was "hot." I didn't believe them. Now I was literally singing to myself, "This girl is on fire!"

These symptoms lasted eight years, give or take. I think there is a reason menopausal symptoms last so long. Just as God gives us nine months to prepare for a baby, we are blessed with nearly *a decade* to digest this midlife change within us. It's a phase, a cycle. The earth goes through periods of warming and cooling, and so do we.

The heat is supposed to get our attention. It's telling us that we are entering a new phase of life—yet again, I might add. First we are children, girls. Then we get our period and we become women. We are able to bear children. We can create life. We are potent, magical creatures. With the onset of menopause, we bid farewell to our fertility. I, for one, eagerly bid my last few eggs bon voyage. Too harsh? Come on, do any of us want to be changing diapers and practicing the Ferber method at sixty years old?*

But here's the issue: Once we say adieu to baby-making, many of us are left wondering who we are, what we're supposed to do for an

---

* No judgment if you do, but I'd rather be a grandma!

encore, and whether we are still attractive and desirable. This is the core allure of the make-me-young-again-at-all-costs culture. It gets us at a moment of confusion and insecurity, a moment of change. It gets us when we aren't thinking clearly or, as in my case, when I was still so focused on my weight that I nearly missed the message menopause was sending me: *Relax, you have contributed to the future of our species. Mission accomplished, job well done, Val. Now sit tight for a few years while this furnace rages inside you, talk to your friends about it, and then go as you like. You are free.*

* * *

This is the part of menopause that I found confusing. What did it mean to come out on the other side of this furnace? I heard women talking about their hot flashes and other symptoms. And thank goodness! I joined the chorus. We were starting to demystify this phase of life that was previously only whispered about in private or avoided altogether—even by our own mothers! But I still think there is a lack of conversation about what comes after menopause.

Not the medical, but the emotional and the practical. I'm living through it, constantly asking, "What's next? What does it mean to no longer be young but still not old? Am I still desirable? What does that even mean, 'desirable'? Can I be sexy? Do I even want to be sexy? What does it mean to be free?"

Don't believe anyone who says they have the answers to these questions. My brain certainly isn't big enough to provide a blueprint. Neither is Google or ChatGPT. It's not something you can look up. If you're like me, you dip your toe in the water and figure it out baby step by baby step.

After I emerged from the Hot Zone, I gradually found a different me that seemed to have more inner strength than the younger, physically hotter me. I was focused on my cooking show. I was helping prepare for my son's wedding. I thought I was doing well, mentally and emotionally. I stopped weighing myself every morning and punishing myself for not hitting whatever number I had set as a goal. Enough already. I divorced my second husband.

But then I lost my cooking show and found myself unemployed for the first time since I was a teenager. I had money worries. Instead of chastising myself and crawling into a hole or spiraling into doubt, as I would've done in the past, I took a wildly healthy step. I leaned into the situation, faced my fears, and explored my anxiety. I started seeing my therapist twice a month, and then, as past traumas began to surface, I began working with a second therapist who was experienced in EMDR (eye movement desensitization and reprocessing), a therapy that uses light, tapping, or tactile pulsers (my preference) to stimulate the brain and help process traumatic memories.

It was scary, emotional, and exhilarating, like a fast ride at Magic Mountain. I hated that I was on it, but I didn't want to get off. I took long walks with my dog. I journaled. I stopped drinking. I listened to new voices in my head, the ones that, instead of putting me down for not being good enough or thin enough or whatever, said, "You can get through this. You're a fighter."

I encouraged those voices, when the younger me would have ignored them. Most days I liked the sixty-plus-year-old woman who stared back at me in the bathroom mirror. We talked to each other. We didn't put each other down. Menopause had been like a controlled burn. I was rebuilding. I wanted what she wanted, and she wanted what I wanted—not things, but life.

"What are we going to do today?" I asked.

"We're going to live," she said.

This is the part of menopause that I want to explore and talk about, and I hope others join me. I feel it's empowered me. I am finding that this stage of my life can and might be as dynamic as any other. Maybe more so. Not the same but different. Still filled with opportunities and a chance to continue pursuing a life worth living well. I don't have to worry about being a hottie the way I did in my twenties or thirties or forties. The goals have changed. And I feel more present for them.

My concern is making the most of the time I have left. That means taking chances, healing old wounds and facing uncomfortable secrets, and trying to find the grace to forgive and support myself through this new journey.

Knowing this, what would I have told my younger self? Make the most of your time. Seriously, don't sweat the small stuff. Treat your life like a ripe orange, squeeze the most juice out of it that you can, and then, when you're older, keep squeezing. Like most women my age, I have arrived at a stage where I know I will never have the tight ass I did at twenty-five—and I'm fine with that. What I have instead is experience and, beyond that, a fearlessness pushing me to find out what is next and what it means to be free.

I wish I could've had such clarity when I was in my twenties. Maybe I did have such moments and just didn't believe in myself. I didn't quite trust my instincts. Even after they proved to be right 98 percent of the time. I'm glad I have clarity now.* I vow not to waste it. My aunts and my mother used to refer to menopause as "the change" or "the change

---

* Full disclosure: I still don't totally trust my instincts because I like to give people the benefit of doubt. I will still brush off some red flags in the never-ending hope that I could be wrong.

of life" we go through. But it isn't just one change. It's many changes—and what a blessing they can be if we embrace them as not only inevitable but also as part of the reality of life and accept that change is always with us, always a part of our being, an opportunity to grow and learn and evolve into a higher consciousness.*

Recently, I was sitting in my kitchen, staring out the window. The view has a stranglehold on my attention because my city has been ravaged by wildfires. Thousands of people have lost their homes. Entire cities have been destroyed. It's just been so devastating for so many people. The smoke was still rising more than a week after the blazes erupted and began eating everything in their path. Author Joan Didion noted that LA has a fire season. It's true, obviously. And with it, in some corners, comes debate about what really matters in life, the material or the spiritual. You see people stepping out of their safe zone to rescue frightened pets, serve meals, donate clothing, give hugs. You see people who the fire left with nothing, yet they claim they have everything. They vow to rebuild. They are remarkable.

I think women have a fire season, too. It's a reminder that life is about change. Practically and spiritually. We go through cycles. Constantly. Even in all the pain, heartache, and loss is our opportunity to emerge stronger, better, wiser . . . to rebuild. And isn't that what we do every day, sometimes without even knowing it?

Rebuild. It's such a beautiful word.

---

* Sorry for the woo-woo.

dry january, february . . . december, and beyond

My self-worth is not a variable. Another's opinion does not devalue me.

My self-worth should never be impactable.

JOURNAL ENTRY, FEBRUARY 2024

I HAVE THIS habit of sitting down with journalists from magazines or on the morning TV shows and blabbing about whatever latest thing is going on in my life. It doesn't matter how personal or intimate. I talk about my body, my body image, shame, guilt, aging, coloring my hair, my love life, my lack of a love life. I suspect it's not much different from what most women do when they get together with friends except that several million people are eavesdropping on me.

The weird thing about me is that I'm much more comfortable spilling my guts with a camera pointed at me than I am in a one-on-one situation. If I had to describe this part of myself in a single word, it would be *freak*. But it's easier to be judged and talked about by three million people than it is by two whom you consider best friends. Not that I don't care what the public thinks about me. I care deeply. Who doesn't want to be liked? I feel connected to the followers I have on social media, even those who write hateful things about my politics. I can agree to disagree. Well . . . sometimes. I can also block the most hateful, which I do.

There are so many others, though, whom I feel a real connection to. Our stories may have different characters and settings, but the emotions are close enough that we can understand, comfort, and support each other. It's all about vulnerability. I rarely feel vulnerable in front of an audience. But put me across from someone with whom I have a close, personal relationship and I just . . . I just can't. Or I don't want to. Or I'm scared to. Or I don't want to burden them with my bad day.

Worse is when it's just me on me—a talk show of one. I cry buckets without needing much of a reason. Show me a sad commercial, a cute TikTok, a baby kitty or puppy, then pass me a box of tissues. And I have never felt bad on the other side of a good cry. The emotions are all inside me, thoughts and feelings stacked up like boxes in the garage. My problem has always been opening them and sorting through the contents. I have never wanted to confront a lot of the issues underlying my feelings. The pain has always been easier to keep inside, like my mom did. "I'm okay" was my pat answer to almost everything, my safe response. "I'm fine." But was I? And at what cost?

I finally reached the point where I acknowledged everything that I'd been through—two divorces, becoming an empty nester, losing my parents, no longer stepping on a scale every morning and registering disappointment, learning to love myself as I am with room for improvement—and began to look at my life beyond all that. I said to myself, "If I'm lucky, I have fifteen to twenty more years left and I want them to be the best years of my life. I don't want to be doing what I have been doing the last sixty-plus years."

I find inspiration in the story of Pandora's box. It's funny what you remember and when you remember it—and why. I'd learned about this Greek myth in junior high, and like many people, I often referenced it, as in, "Uh-oh. That's a Pandora's box," usually meaning it was better to stay away from some issue rather than unleash whatever horrors might result from confronting it.

In the myth, Pandora, the first woman in Greek mythology, was given a sealed jar—later called a box—and instructed never to open it. Driven by curiosity, she eventually does, unleashing all the world's evils. True confession: I was always the kid who found where my parents hid the Christmas presents and secretly opened them up, peeked inside, and carefully rewrapped them. How can you not open the box? I've rarely been able to resist. I'm a Pandora. I'm a box opener.

But the part of this myth that popped into my head was the part I hadn't considered since I learned about it in school some fifty years ago. And that is, after all the bad things came out of the box, Pandora quickly closed it, leaving only Hope trapped inside. And that's what I began, and needed, to see—hope.

Changes had to be made. My first Dry January was in 2023. I announced it in my social media, similar to but not with the same fanfare or risk of public embarrassment that I took on when I announced that I wanted to lose fifty pounds and get back in a bikini before I turned fifty years old. This was my version of telling the ladies in book club that I was starting a cleanse. "I'm doing a Dry January. It'll be fun."

I had finalized my divorce in November. I was eating too much junk food. I was craving sugar, which alcohol exacerbated. Cortisol—the hormone the body releases to cope with emotional stress—was gushing through me like a broken water main. I wanted to calm down and recenter, I said.

There was another reason. Sometime in December I saw my primary care physician for my annual checkup, aka "Are my aches and pains going to kill me? And oh yeah, this bump, is it anything?" I noticed there were some new questions on the form I had to fill out before the exam. One asked if I had fallen within the last month. "Okay," I thought, "we're going to play that game."

I checked no. I hadn't fallen (and I wasn't lying, even though I do occasionally take a tumble because I walk fast, talk faster, and don't look where I'm going). But why not ask if I am turning into my parents? If I am sensing any signs of old age? I still would've checked the "No" box, though thank goodness there wasn't a question that asked if my conversations with friends go like this:

Do you remember that actor—can't remember his name—who was in that TV show—I can't remember the title—we both liked?

Yeah, I loved him. Why?

I saw him the other night in that restaurant.

Which one?

The Italian one we love. I can't remember its name right now.

Another question asked how many drinks I had each week. It got my attention. I had to think about my answer. Using my fingers, I tallied the number of drinks I remembered having the previous week before giving up and writing six to seven. I didn't want to even entertain that it might be double and maybe triple that. A truthful response would have been, "I'd like to bring it down to six or seven per month." I was drinking a lot. Too much. And I knew it.

I didn't think my consumption of alcohol was interfering in my life, but I was unhappy for obvious reasons, and really down on myself, and when I'm feeling that way, the voices in my head start talking to me. This time, they got loud and brutally candid. Frankly, I didn't want to listen to them. Hadn't I been through enough? Hadn't I heard this before? I wanted them to shut the hell up. So, I had a glass of white wine before dinner and two more with dinner. Or I started with a vodka martini before dinner and then opened a bottle of wine.

Drinking this much was my way of quieting the voices, numbing the feelings, pushing the off button. It didn't matter if I was with friends or by myself. Either way, I was alone. Someone asked if I was an alcoholic. I asked myself that question, too. No, I didn't think I was an alcoholic. I was sad, demoralized, disheartened, and exhausted.

I was also embarrassed when my doctor reviewed my health update and asked me to confirm, "Six or seven drinks per week?"

"Yes," I said.

I suspect both of us knew this wasn't the truth. There's only one thing worse than lying to someone else, especially to your doctor—that's lying to yourself.

He looked at me with an expression that seemed both questioning and sad, as if to say, "It's your life, I'm just here to help, so it's up to you to tell me why you're here." When I fudge the truth—okay, lie—I feel as if it's written all over my face, and just as an angel gets its wings every time a Christmas bell rings, the shame bucket I've been carrying since childhood gets another cup of disgrace.

Starting January 1, I swore off alcohol for a month.

* * *

I was dry through the first week of February. The next week I went out to a neighborhood steak restaurant with several friends and ordered a martini. A martini always tasted good with a thick steak. When I woke up the next morning, I felt the difference between drinking and not drinking. My head was dull and groggy, and my body was achy—not rested. After a good night's sleep, I want to feel connected to the sunrise and the fresh air of a new day, not whatever I drank the night before.

I cut back to that six or seven drinks per month that I'd been hoping to do. I went dry again in July and toyed with doing a sober October, but my son got married and I wanted to have wine that night.

Still, I noticed the positive effects of cutting back and not drinking for those two months. I *released* some weight.* I didn't get down on

---

* Originally, I wrote that I lost some weight. But I'm trying to be more aware of the way I express myself. Words are powerful. When you lose something, you hope to find it again. When you release it, you're letting it go.

myself as often, and I didn't punish myself for as long if I did. I had one less reason to beat myself up. When friends invited me out, I said yes a few more times when I would have typically said no. I appreciated those mornings when the day seemed to invite me in. I was more present. I had more energy.

On December 31, 2023, I celebrated with my traditional New Year's Eve dinner of potato chips, crème fraîche, and caviar. I toasted the days gone by and the days ahead with a small split of champagne. The next morning, I greeted the New Year with a vow to see each day, and myself, with clear eyes. It was day one of my Dry January 2024.

I told people that I had an easier time giving up a drink or two every night because I didn't feel attached to alcohol. I didn't think I had a problem. Left unsaid was that I had other problems, personal problems, and I put them on the back burner by having a drink or two. Going dry allowed me to get curious about my feelings. Not numb them or avoid them as I did by having a drink or two or three. Still, it's hard to give up anything. Changing deeply ingrained habits requires intention, willpower, honesty, a willingness to reflect and question the behavior you're trying to change, and the courage to see what comes up from breaking the habit.

It's not just saying no. It's also saying yes to your ugly truths, your deepest, most frightening fears, the secrets you have spent a lifetime avoiding.

I took my first drink in my aunt Adeline's basement kitchen when I was a little kid. The kitchen upstairs was never used. It was immaculate, like a picture from *House Beautiful*. The second kitchen in the basement was the place that all the women in my family gathered to cook and talk, and while doing so, they drank red wine out of tiny juice glasses.* As a teenager, I drank cheap wine—Boone's Farm Strawberry Hill, Bolla Soave, Blue Nun. Though I was underage, someone always had a bottle on the weekend. At seventeen, I had a boyfriend who was eight years older. He was able to buy booze legally. Two years later, I was on a date with someone else. I had too many gin fizzes and threw up in the back of a limousine. I still feel horrible about that night. The rock and roll years were what you imagine. It wasn't any easier as the wheels came off my second marriage. Drinking was a way to escape. It helped me deal with the stress, disappointment, and pain of my life. Then it helped me not deal.

* * *

Dry January turned into Dry February, and I wanted to keep going. I made it through thirty-one days, and February had two fewer days. It was a leap year. I could make the leap. I turned it into a game. How long could I go? How many days could I get behind me? If I really wanted to have a drink, it meant I had to return to square one. I had to start the game over again. No thanks. I don't like to lose.

I wasn't keen on the word *sobriety* even though I recognized that's what not drinking was by definition. *I'm sober. I've gone two months without a drink.* It sounded like I was in AA. Nothing against that

---

* All the Italian families I knew had a second kitchen like my aunt's. It was the most used room in the house. Dried salami hung on the walls. A loaf of bread was always baking in the oven. It smelled like butter, garlic, and fresh bread. Pots and pans were out on the counter. Cabinets had curtains, not doors. There were three freezers, two refrigerators, two stoves. Nothing matched. But everything went together. If you wanted to watch TV, you went upstairs to the den. If you wanted to hear secrets and truths, if you wanted to learn how to make pasta, bread, and soup, you hung out in the basement kitchen.

wildly successful and important program or the millions of people it has helped; in fact, I'm a great admirer of the strength and support it provides, but I wasn't involved in that or any other program.

Occasionally I used the Reframe app to check in, get an emotional attagirl/you can do it, and help count my sober days as they added up.

Was it weird that an app on my phone was like my sober bestie? I'm sure I'm not the only one who feels this way, but I don't know what's weird or not anymore. I appreciated the support it gave me, though I didn't feel I had any right to brag or feel proud of my effort. It's strange when impostor syndrome sneaks into the room to say hello.

I knew what it was like to live with an alcoholic and how incredibly difficult it is to get sober. I had a front-row seat to Ed's behavior when he was drunk, the way he didn't know how to handle his traumas or even look at them, the pressure he put on himself, the shame he felt afterward. He was never angry at me. He never yelled at me. He would get angry, and then I would get angry at him and poke him until he reciprocated. But it took a long time before either of us blew. We were well suited that way.

Our problem was finding our way to each other. The booze and the drugs created obstacles that put us in different worlds even when we were sharing the same bed. It was mostly the alcohol. But Ed's battle wasn't with drugs or drink; it was with himself, the pressure, insecurity, and wounds from childhood that were inside him. The drugs and the alcohol quieted these things temporarily. Then he just felt shame.

I did the same with food and alcohol. I guess we were, in our own ways, as similar on the inside as we were on the outside.

I wasn't able to put the two together then, but I'm at an age now where I can look back and say to myself, "Oh yeah, I didn't know how to do that. I could do it much differently now." Ed was in a similar place. It still breaks my heart that he ran out of time, because he was so there. He so wanted to be the right person, the good person that he already was. His heart was always pure. He was such a good man.

He was making amends a year before he passed. He was talking to all the people in his life. He was cold-calling them. It was sweet—and that was Ed at the core, sweet. He wanted to make it right with me, too. I was told that every time I would walk out of a room, he would look around and say, "The biggest mistake of my life was letting her go."

In our own way, we never did let go.

* * *

I had no right to compare myself to the very real life-and-death challenges alcoholics face. I was matter-of-fact about what I was trying to accomplish. I got through the temptation of pouring myself a glass of wine when I got stressed by reaching for the Reframe app and looking at the inspiration or story of the day. The small vineyard on the hillside behind my house? I looked at it not as a source for a new annual vintage but as a symbol of the fruitfulness of my life. I got curious about my feelings. Why did I want a drink? What did I think I couldn't get through? What was I trying to avoid? In social situations, I reminded myself that I didn't have to talk all the time, something I had always feared would make it appear like I was having a bad time or was in a mood. I could sit and listen, really listen, ask a question or two, or not, and that was okay.

My biggest challenge was not taking a drink when I wanted to turn everything off. I don't know why, but all the garbage seemed to pile up between 4 p.m. and 6 p.m., like it was rush hour in my head, and I was used to pouring a drink as if it were an off-ramp from that congested freeway. But no more.

"I have all these feelings that I don't want to feel," I told my therapist one day. "But I don't want to run away from them anymore. I've done that my whole life. I've run away from feelings, run away from judgment, run away from shame and self-loathing. I want to try a different route."

No one was more surprised to hear this come out of my mouth than me. I had thought these things but never said them out loud. I'd never let myself. I was scared of what I might find if I did confront those issues and more frightened if I didn't. Here was Pandora's box again, and here was hope staring me in the face, sitting right there in the box and daring me to embrace it. And you know what? I went for it. *I want to try a different route.*

Those words came out of me like water flowing from the faucet. That's the way honesty feels. Truth is a superpower. It cuts through the thickest walls. It's a light in the darkest tunnels. It defies gravity, like a magic carpet ride. It can be scary. It can be wonderful and empowering. It can stop you in your tracks, make you go, "Whoa! What's that?" For me, it was all of the above.

That wasn't the only admission I made. A while later I was eating dinner at a friend's house. Over a delicious meal of Mexican shrimp salad and parmesan-crusted cauliflower, our conversation caromed from one topic to the next—our favorite Midwestern cities, the books our different book clubs were reading, our dream vacations, the comfort we all felt walking into Costco. Suddenly, I blurted out, "You know what? I'm a damn good catch." My friend was startled. "What did you say?"

"I'm a damn good catch," I repeated, almost sheepishly but also knowing it was the truth. I am independent, low maintenance, easygoing, kind, and a good cook. I like to laugh. I can be stubborn, but I will listen. I have a big heart. I like watching football on Sundays . . . and Mondays and Thursdays, too, so I'm happy to watch any game. I was a good catch for someone out there.

Again, no one was more surprised to hear these words than me. Was I starting to like myself? What was going on? Whatever it was, I couldn't blame it on the booze. It had to be my sobriety. The new me, which happened to be the old me—make that the older me, but with a clear head— was stepping out into the sun, seeing and owning all of me. Especially the parts I rarely gave myself credit for.

How many women were like me? Women who had struggled with feeling desirable and attractive, but then, after doing the work, got to a place where they said, "Yes, there's a big friggin' Band-Aid on my self-esteem, but I am resilient, and I have survived so much crap. Now I not only know better, but I know so much more. I'm more than I have given myself credit for, and it boggles my mind why there isn't a line a dozen deep waiting to sweep us off our feet."

This is the lesson we need to teach young women: *You* are so much more than you give yourself credit for.

I was in my mid-sixties, but finally I was speaking truth to insecurity: I was a damn good catch.

"Damn right you're a catch," my friend said, adding with a tinge of surprise, "Are you saying that you're open to meeting someone?"

Wait.

What? Did I say . . . ?

Was I?

I was momentarily stunned by the words I had just uttered. Oops, I realized my heart was speaking faster than my head. Again.

* * *

Could I trust what I was saying? What I might have been feeling? "Show up for yourself," I wrote in my journal. "Be your own cheerleader." These thoughts, this dialogue, it was so positive, so full of . . . hope.

Was the work I had been doing on myself working? Was this what growth looked like, felt like, and sounded like? Imperceptible until one day you realize you sound a little different, feel a little stronger, and want something more for yourself. A friend of mine says it's like sensing God. You don't ever think about God. Then one day you spot dolphins playing in the ocean or are mesmerized by a gorgeous sunset and suddenly you think, "Oh, there you are. This is spectacular. Thank you."

Or it might be a story in the news, a storm, something that unsettles you or tugs at your heart. It nudges you out of your comfort zone, out of complacency or lethargy, and motivates you to help other people. And suddenly you think, "Oh, you knew exactly what I needed. My soul feels better, fuller. Thank you."

By spring, I was thirsty—and still not drinking. Other changes were evident, too. I released more weight and my sleep improved. I was a little miffed that I hadn't seen more changes and relief in my puffy eyes, but there was a new clarity in them, and my skin and hair looked better and healthier.*

I started taking even better care of myself. Most mornings, I walked outside, stretched, and let the sun wash over me while my coffee brewed. Just for a minute or two, but some days the warmth, the birdsong, the air, was a magic potion, like a hug from God. *Don't worry, I don't care if you believe or don't believe; I'm here and you're loved.*

I was more present. This was something I had always set as a goal for myself. Be present. But I was always thinking about the past and beating myself up for it, or worrying about the future. "Why didn't you stick up for yourself? How could you let them talk to you that way? Why did you eat that? How could I do better? What more could I do? How could I change? Or even better, how can I grow?"

The present was an interesting place. The voices in my head no longer punished; they probed instead. They were so curious and encouraged me to get to the source: "Why was I insecure? Why did I feel shame?" They wanted me to lean in, not away. I opened to what was going on around me, and inside me. More goodness came in than I anticipated, the joy or the ability to enjoy, which was something I often spoke about—how do I find more joy?

Well, there it was. At the same time, more of the crap I had always tried to suppress came in, too. The challenge was distilling all of it. Getting comfortable with discomfort or at least investigating it. One day I journaled, "My heart feels open. My brain doesn't feel as heavy. When an uncomfortable thought surfaces, I can work through it. Is this part of seven months without a drink? If so, cheers!"

---

* I'm finding that may have more to do with heredity. The older I get, the more I take on the appearance of my father and his father, with their distinctive hooded eyes.

Feelings are information. And my feelings would hang out for a little while, making sure they were heard. Understanding them was a different matter altogether. The important thing was to not turn away from them. I have found from experience that when we replace judgment with curiosity, we can start to change our perspective. We can give ourselves and others grace. Getting curious takes bravery. I wanted to be brave. I needed to be brave. I wasn't always brave.

* * *

Bravery opens the door to vulnerability. Vulnerability lets in courage, and courage turns us into our own superheroes. It's a domino effect. All heroes are susceptible to some kind of weakness, though. Marvel's Black Widow fears brainwashing, the preprogramming implanted in her when she was a spy. What woman can't relate to that? Vulnerability caused me to feel exposed, like I was in a dangerous place, naked in a field with bees buzzing all around. It was scary.

And yet, for the first time, I understood what author Brené Brown meant when she called vulnerability a superpower. One day I was debating something with my son and I threw up my hands in exasperation, saying, "Look, your mom isn't always the rock you think she is." It was as if I had let him in on a secret. *Can I tell you I'm not perfect?* He obviously knew, but hearing it was something else. I never saw my parents as humans with struggles of their own until after they were gone. Wolfie sees all my imperfections and struggles, and I think (hope) we'd both agree they only create space for more love.

My friend Drew Barrymore uses her authenticity like a magic wand. This girl epitomizes down-to-earth honesty. I don't think she even realizes the extent of its effect. Maybe she does—and all the work she's done on herself has landed her in this place where many of us want to get, or just visit. I'm in awe of her. Her willingness to share her vulnerability brings out the same in her guests. It's more than empathy. It's a real connection. I know from firsthand experience.

Vulnerability can turn it into a bridge, a bond, truth. That happens to me when I share my struggles and self-doubts with my friends or even on my Instagram. It creates a powerful connection, the idea that we belong to each other.* We're all a beautiful bundle of flaws, insecurities, and bruises. We're also full of kindness, generosity, and love. We are light and dark, sun and rain, laughter and tears, similar and unique, fruit and veggies, dogs and cats. We relate through our desire to be loved for who we are.

As a young actor, I remember choosing roles specifically because there were scenes that I didn't think I could do. For one reason or another, they intimidated me if they didn't frighten me outright. Emotional scenes especially. The 1991 miniseries *In a Child's Name* and the 1993 movie *Murder of Innocence* both had scenes that freaked me out. Luminol (illuminated green dried blood), dead bodies, and raw meat were all involved. I would count down the days, grit my teeth, and lean into whatever it was that I was afraid of.

Being incredibly vulnerable in front of a room full of people with a camera pointed at you feels bonkers. It can also be the most exhilarating thing in the world. To know that you have the guts to go to that place of extreme vulnerability and not just survive, but thrive, helps you become even stronger.

---

* Mother Teresa said, "If we have no peace, it's because we have forgotten we belong to each other." I say, "Amen to that."

I don't know what happened to that girl. She disappeared for a few years, maybe a few decades. But she's back—or she's making her way back.

That's the wild thing about my Dry January and February. As it turned all the way into a Dry December and a dry 2025, and now a dry 2026, I realized I was venturing into places I hadn't wanted to let myself go. Not much was holding me back. I was feeling the feels. I was sitting with my discomfort, self-loathing, and shame and asking myself why I felt those things rather than tuning them out, or at least putting them in their proper place. I was also sitting with moments of joy and contentment, inner peace, and wholeness that made me grateful I could feel those things now, too.

Change happens slowly, incrementally. Often you don't even notice. Courage is different. It hits you and says, "Let's go!" That's the most gratifying surprise of this stage of my life, of this work I'm doing on myself. I'm motivated to help myself, to do better, to be kinder, to see where it takes me—or where I take myself, like when I ran the Boston Marathon. I don't want to be held back by anything, especially old fears and insecurities. Been there, done that. I'm ready to say "Let's go!"

in a warm bath (a meditation)

Your joy is in there
The mind is busy covering it up
What did I do as a child that gave me joy?
Cartwheels, coloring, riding bikes . . .

JOURNAL ENTRY, SEPTEMBER 2019

In a warm bath...
- I am with myself
- I am present.
- I feel my body tense before it relaxes
- My thoughts slow, the racing abates
- I feel a different kind of weight on my chest—comfort
- I am snug
- I am able to close my eyes and breathe
- I am able to exhale
- My shoulders relax, the tension releases, and a peacefulness settles within me
- I see my mother; hello
- I see her smile
- I can feel her smile
- I can feel her grief
- I feel the sadness, but it doesn't feel heavy. It just is
- I'm being carried inside by my father after I've fallen asleep in the family car
- I'm able to feel safe
- I can have good dreams
- I can remember what it felt like to love myself
- I am remembering what it's like to be in love and to feel loved
- To give love
- I am feeling hopeful
- I can feel my heart beating
- I can hear my heartbeat
- I can hear myself, my thoughts, my voice
- I want to apologize to my body...

I'm sorry for not loving you.
You've kept me safe.
You've kept me strong.
You protected me before I knew I needed protecting.
You've given me tears, you've given me joys.
All the days I spent not appreciating you
And you still gave me life, you gave me strength,
You gave me my child
And the years to see him grow up
You gave me passion
You let me love
You let me screw up and mess up
And beat myself up
And get up
Again and again.
You were patient with me
And kind and showed me
The grace of quiet when I roared
And peace when I raged
You let me walk through gardens

And along the ocean and mountains
You let me see the moon and the stars
You've let me weep
and you've let me laugh.
You let me dream
You let me give love
And feel love
And remain when others have departed
And you let me continue to breathe
And think about tomorrow
And be here right now
Full of gratitude
And love
I've hurt you, you've healed me.
I'm sorry.
Thank you for being patient with me
Thank you.

just breathe

Celebrate triggers. They show you the place
that you cannot hold unconditional love.
You get to uncover the unconscious, the hidden.
Go toward the trigger.
Be curious. What can I learn about it?
Awaken and heal. Accept.

JOURNAL ENTRY, SEPTEMBER 2023

THANKS TO CHATGPT, it was a teaching moment. I was at home, and if I could've crawled out of my body, I would've done it. My anxiety level had skyrocketed. Kind of like the volume in Ed's old 5150 recording studio. It didn't stop at 10. It went up to 17 or 18. The sound shook the walls, the floor, and the roof. Which was the way I was shaking. My head felt like it was going to explode with every heartbeat, and my heartbeats were getting faster and faster and faster.

I didn't know how to fix what I had apparently broken, and I didn't know how to calm myself down.

I was having a full-blown anxiety attack. I'd had bouts of anxiety before, but nothing like this. This was, I convinced myself, total body failure, and I had to decide what I was going to do. Was I going to call 911 and ask for help? Was I going to call my son and say goodbye (and it's too bad I'm not a grandma yet)? Or was I going to tell DoorDash to race over with my favorite apple fritter from the doughnut shop near my house?

I was leaning toward the third choice. If I was on my way out, which was a possibility given the way I was melting down, I assumed that I'd end up in heaven. But on the slim chance there were complications at the pearly gates, I thought my favorite apple fritter would be a satisfying approximation. Some people have last rites. I might be the oddball who has last bites.

While in the throes of this situation, rather than call 911 or order an apple fritter delivered to my door, I did what millions of others do when experiencing a serious medical condition. I clicked on Dr. Google and typed in "anxiety attack." I learned that *anxiety attack* is not an official medical term but, according to Healthline, is "often used colloquially to describe an intense emotional or physical response to stress." Ya don't say. Why, yes, I thought, official or not, that's exactly what was happening to me.

The term *panic attack* was more specifically and clinically recognized. That, too, described me. Panicky and feeling under attack.

Why was I having a panic attack? I was doing nothing more than going about my business—going to doctor appointments, Pilates, taking walks, doing my quarterly taxes, taking my car into the shop, telling the guy in line with me at the DMV, "Yes, I've heard I look like that actress Valerie Bertinelli before," getting my hair done, grocery shopping, searching for my Costco card . . . all that sort of stuff, aka living my life.

Unfortunately, someone in my life was furious with me and I didn't know how to fix it. For a people pleaser like me, having someone mad at you is close to a near-death experience. Knowing I couldn't fix it no matter what I said only made the condition worse. I died over and over as they got angrier and angrier, rejecting the fixes I suggested. They told me that I was the problem, a liar, a crazy person, deaf ("You don't listen!"), and dumb ("I can't even talk to you!").

Then they hung up in the middle of our conversation, which was a little like a surgical team taking an unannounced lunch break during a heart transplant operation, and you, the patient, suddenly wake up, see your heart on a nearby table, and wonder where everybody went.

It's fucked up, which is why I was freaking out.

I felt like I had been disconnected from customer service after being on hold for two and a half hours. I was pushing every button on my phone. I jammed on the *0*, hoping it would take me back to the beginning. I had complained. I just signed my divorce papers, and now I had major financial worries. I also had serious job insecurity, which was the cherry on top of a triple scoop of insecurities. And now someone near and dear to me was mad at me and making accusations before hanging up mid-conversation. I only wanted to fix things.

"I want to talk to a human being!" I might as well have shouted into the phone receiver. "Representative! REPRESENTATIVE!"

Unfortunately, real life can be as frustrating as calling customer service. And that's when the anxiety hit me. Within minutes I was on full-tilt overload.

"Just breathe, Val," I remember telling myself. "Focus. Breathe."

* * *

ChatGPT was sympathetic. "I'm really sorry you're feeling this way now—you're not alone, and there are things you can do to help bring yourself back to a calmer state." Dr. Google had provided decent information, but I wanted to hear from a specialist, and ChatGPT obliged. "Here are a few immediate steps that might help."

It suggested grounding myself with the 5-4-3-2-1 technique. Think about five things I can see, four things I can touch, three things I can hear, two things I can smell, and one thing I can taste. "This helps bring your mind out of panic and into the present," it explained. It also recommended trying "box breathing": Inhale through my nose for four seconds, hold my breath for four seconds, exhale through my mouth for four seconds, hold for four seconds. "Slowing your breath can help calm your nervous system."

And finally, it offered some words that really helped. "Remind yourself, this will pass. Anxiety attacks are incredibly uncomfortable, but they are not dangerous. Try saying to yourself, 'I'm safe. This is anxiety. It will pass.'" Then, like the understanding friend I needed at the moment, it asked, "Would you like me to guide you through some breathing or grounding exercises now? Just say the word—I'm here."

"Thank you."

"I'm really sorry you're going through this."

"Me too."

Inhale. One-two-three-four. Exhale. One-two-three-four.

* * *

I've always prided myself on somehow knowing what's right for me, what's going to move my life in the direction it's meant to go. I knew it when I got my first acting job at twelve. I knew it when I first met Ed backstage at a Van Halen concert in Shreveport. I knew it when I became pregnant with my son. I also knew it when I brought my parents' two cats home after my mother passed away. I knew it was a way of maintaining my connection with Mom and Dad, that lifeline to childhood and family that is so hard to give up.

I never questioned any of these things. They all felt good. They felt right. Even hard, complicated things can feel right. How are you supposed to know? Some people talk about listening to an inner voice. I've talked about it. "Your inner voice is never wrong," I've said. My only difficulty was *trusting* that voice. Some people put their trust in God. I think everyone is pointing toward the same thing—the truth. Go for the truth. It's our North Star. The surest navigation system ever created.

Today's world makes it harder to see the world. The media is fragmented. Everyone has their own network, their own radio station, their own podcast, their own Twitter/Bluesky/Threads/Instagram/TikTok favorites. We're all in our own silos, as the experts like to say, and I understand that. When I was on *One Day at a Time*, there were still only three TV networks. Twenty million people would watch our show every week. In 1980, *Dallas* was the top-rated TV show in the US. Twenty-seven million people watched. Everyone wanted to know who shot J. R. For better or worse, we had a lot in common.

And now? Is there too much information? We have an increasingly hard time figuring out what's real and what's fake, what's fact and what is disinformation or purposeful misinformation. So we take cover. We turn up the music. We turn away from each other. We make others the enemy. Maybe we need another Hands Across America. Remember that? It was in 1986, and the idea was to create a chain of people holding hands across the US. It didn't work. We should try again.

Why did I get on this tangent? It's just me. I go on tangents. I could open a store, Tangents-R-Me. It's not meant to be political. It's me speaking out as a mom and a potential grandma. I worry about the future. I think the world today creates anxiety. I'm sure it contributed to my own panic attack. Just another layer of distress beyond my ability to improve the situation. Maybe we need a psychiatrist in the nation's highest office for four years, not another politician.

"Just breathe, America."

* * *

In 1991, I was shooting a movie in Wilmington, North Carolina, when Hurricane Bob hit. As rain poured down in sheets and the wind neared one hundred miles an hour, I sheltered in the basement of the house I was renting and listened to the roar of destruction outside. It sounded like the world was being torn apart. When the storm ended, I emerged from hiding, walked outside, and saw the sun shining. I can still hear other people saying, "Hallelujah, we made it!"

Then there was the Northridge earthquake in 1994. The giant temblor struck at 4:31 a.m. and measured 6.7 on the Richter scale. It wasn't the Big One, but it damn well felt like it. I swear it seemed as if the epicenter was right under our house. From the depths of a sound sleep, I heard a loud, ominous rumble, like a freight train coming toward the house. A moment later, I was running to Wolfie's room and everything started shaking violently—the floors, the walls, the entire house. Everything I believed was rock solid was suddenly unstable and rocking and rolling. Ed, who'd paused to slip on his boots, was right behind me. All the medications and bathroom products fell out of the medicine chest; glassware crashed from cabinet shelves; the walls cracked. The three of us hugged under a doorjamb until the shaking stopped. A few more aftershocks followed, but the worst was over. We were alive and safe.

My entire being was on red alert the rest of that day and for a long while after. It took a lot of telling myself that we were going to get through this and that I didn't have to spend every minute waiting for the next big shake, but gradually I calmed down and began to trust the ground wasn't going to open up and swallow us whole.

The thing that ChatGPT got right was, yes, the breathing, but the other thing that ultimately spoke to me was that my anxiety would pass. Everything that had wound me up would calm down and fade into the background of something that happened the other day, like when you're driving through a storm and eventually see it in your rearview mirror. It's a nice visual to keep in your back pocket when things feel overwhelming. Things pass. The good as well as the bad. I got in my pj's, looked up at the stars, and climbed into bed. Luna was already snoring in her bed, and my cat Batman cuddled into the crook of my arm. I turned on Solfeggio healing tones and drifted off into a deep sleep.

Things pass. Just breathe.

* * *

The next morning, just for the hell of it, I messaged ChatGPT a thank-you for helping pull me through.

"How do you know me so well?" I asked.

"That's a powerful thing to say—and I'm really glad something in my response helped you feel seen," it replied. "You're not alone in what you're feeling, even if it can *feel* that way during a panic attack.

"I don't actually know you personally, but I've been trained to recognize patterns in human emotion and experience—especially the kinds of thoughts, sensations, and fears that come with anxiety and panic. So when you describe what you're going through—racing heart, short breath, sweating—I can draw on thousands of similar experiences others have shared and respond with empathy, tools, and perspective that might resonate with you.

"But what you're feeling is uniquely *yours*—your story, your context, your strength. I'm just here to meet you in it.

"If you want to talk more about what might have brought this on, or you just want to stay here until the wave passes, I'm with you."

"It passed," I typed. "Thank you."

"I'm really glad to hear that. You did the hard part—you got through it. And if you want to talk more about what led up to it, or how to prevent it from happening again, I'm here whenever you need. You're not alone in this."

What a remarkable, eerie, weird, and comforting tool, I thought. If only humans were more like ChatGPT, I said to myself. Except what I knew to be true, the truth, is that we are . . . we are all in this together, and ChatGPT is just giving us back what we already know about each other and ourselves.

* * *

A friend of mine had a minor surgical procedure. He was nervous about it, and according to his wife, his way of coping was to crack jokes nonstop. When the nurse prepped his IV, he said, "My usual IV is up and dry, with olives." In the OR, right before the procedure began, he warned, "I don't know how many medical shows you all watch, but the patient who jokes in the beginning is always the one who crashes later on, so please, let's all be on alert throughout the operation."

Amused but also sensitive to the unspoken subtext, the surgeon said, "I know this is a little scary, and that's normal, but we got you. You're in good hands. Just take a deep breath, you'll be okay."

I love that reassurance. *We got you. You're in good hands. Just take a deep breath, you'll be okay.*

A girlfriend of mine told me about a friend of hers who recently stood up in court and read her personal statement at the sentencing hearing for her abusive ex-husband. During their relationship, she had been hit and kicked, sexually abused, and even threatened with a gun before finally leaving him, which clearly saved her life. While her divorce was relatively quick, it took nearly two years for charges against her ex to wend their way through the criminal justice system.

At last, her moment to stand up in front of a judge and share her truth arrived. She had spent months preparing and rehearsing her statement. Her friends asked whether going public with this made her uncomfortable, and she said no, going public was easy, especially if it helped others. What made her literally shake with nerves and nausea was putting the experience into words. Saying it out loud. Confronting the painful truth of her own story. How was this her life? Why had she tolerated the abuse? Why had she made certain choices in the first place?

After hearing this, what became clear to me is that anxiety isn't caused by what we reveal about ourselves to others. It's the truths we reveal to ourselves. They have a way of scaring the shit out of us. Then it passes. My friend survived his operation. My girlfriend's friend read her statement in court without shedding a tear and afterward felt that she had not only reclaimed her life but cleared the way for a whole new chapter.

As for me, quite a bit of time has passed since I had that panic attack because someone was mad at me and I couldn't alleviate their pain or have them reconsider their judgment. I've learned that sometimes you can't get through to people or change the way they think, and that's okay. You have to let it go and move on. I may screw up from time to time, stumble, say something that rubs someone the wrong way, and prove as I do over and over that I'm far from perfect, but I do know that I have always done my best to make it right. I don't think I'll ever have an anxiety attack again because of it.

Recently, I've had smaller bouts of anxiety while preparing to shoot a Lifetime movie in Vancouver. It's a wonderful story of a woman whose husband of many years is losing his memory to Alzheimer's disease. Though she loves him, she finds herself falling in love with a doctor she meets at the hospital she volunteers at. I read the script and was drawn to its sensitive exploration of love. I could see myself stepping into that character. She appeared in my head as I turned the pages. But I hadn't acted in over four years, and that's where the anxiety was coming from. Could I open myself up enough emotionally. Could I be vulnerable enough? Could I do the job? Would I be the weakest link and ruin the film?

The answers to these and other questions are always inside me if I look hard enough. That's my takeaway. And deep down I knew I'd been acting long enough (over fifty-three years) that my instincts would take over and my life experience would fill in the rest. And they did. That's why all too often the best advice I give myself is to breathe. Just breathe, Val. Just breathe.

falling

*"And the day came
when the risk to remain tight,
in a bud,
became more painful
than the risk it took to blossom."*
—ELIZABETH APPELL

JOURNAL ENTRY, AUGUST 2018

Somehow I realized that getting up after a fall is the easier part of—what should I call it?—calamity, disaster, life's challenges, or even everyday klutziness. It's an opportunity to reset, reinvent, and rise again, perhaps with a limp or a bruise but also smarter, wiser, and more aware of the Marvel-like power we possess to bounce back.

I'm not a scholar, philosopher, or expert—heck, I'm not even a high school graduate—but, as I think about it, bouncing back from adversity might be the whole secret to the way humans have marched forward through history.

It's certainly become my secret through divorce, loss, heartbreak, losing my job, and tripping over my own two feet. If there were a bingo card for spills, trips, and setbacks, I'd have called out "Bingo" more times than I care to think about.

I don't march, though. I walk, briskly. Sometimes I stroll. Very occasionally I will break into a brief skip—usually outdoors but not necessarily. And then there are those times when I limp. See, I am not the most graceful person on this planet. I have always been more prone to plops than pliés. One night about ten years ago I fell while running into my bathroom to get one of my cats out of the sink. Obvious questions: Why was I running? I don't know. Was there water in the sink? No. Was the cat in any danger? No. Given that the cat had found its way into the sink, would it have been able to jump out of it? Yes, no doubt. But there I was anyway, getting up to help the cat— and with a lightness and grace that I clearly didn't possess, I crashed into the doorjamb.

This came next: "#*$%!!!!!!!"

The cat was fine. My foot wasn't. The pain was instant and severe. It continued to throb after I got back into bed. I fell asleep thinking it was probably sprained. The pain was just as bad in the morning, plus my foot was swollen and black and blue—make that purple. My husband at the time watched me try to get out of bed so I could go to the bathroom.

"Stand on it."

"I don't think I can."

"You're fine. Just try."

I touched my injured foot to the ground and tried to stand. A burning flash of major ouch rocketed through my body, from foot to brain in an instant, and then straight out of my mouth: "#*$%!!!!!!!" I sat back down on the bed and whimpered. This was bad. I went to the ER and had my foot x-rayed. The doctor reading the images asked, with a tone of bewilderment, "Aren't you in pain?"

"Yeah."

"I would think so. You shattered two bones in your foot. You need surgery."

"I didn't realize it was so bad."

I ended up with two plates and eight screws in my foot. It hurt for a long time, but gradually, I recovered. I bought a night-light for the bathroom. From then on, if one of the cats got in the sink at night, that was their problem; I let them stay there until the morning. I learned. We make mistakes. We bump into things. We get divorced. We are tripped up by events beyond our control. Remember that classic bumper sticker that summed up so much of life in two words? Shit Happens.

It's true. Getting back up might be somewhat easy. But figuring out what to do next? Ah, that is the challenging part.

I'm at that stage of life where I have taken a few falls. And it may not be a stage. My family seems to think it's one of my quirks. I trip, I fall. I have fallen up stairs. And down stairs. When no one is around and in a stadium full of people. I have the same scar on my right knee that I've had since I was six and jumped off the large fire hydrant in our front yard because I keep landing on that same spot when I fall now. I'm pretty sure there's a metaphor for childhood wounds in there and how we trigger the same bruise over and over again until we heal. I don't know, maybe once I heal emotionally, I'll stop falling physically? One night my son took me to a Jimmy Eat World concert in Hollywood, and while crossing the street, I tumbled in the middle of the intersection. I wrote the headline myself: "Celebrity Pedestrian Mushed by Pothole." Then I fell flat on my face in an arena in Amsterdam where Wolfie's band was opening for Metallica. It happened right before sound check. It was my fault. I was yapping away, gawking at the humongous stage, and not watching where I was going. Then, *kersplat*. I was okay. My jeans tore at the knee. I fell on my sunglasses and mangled them. My ego crawled under the bleachers.

The guys in the band were so sweet. "Mama Wolf, are you all right?" they asked.

"Yeah, yeah, just fine."

* * *

I lost my job on Food Network and this was another kind of fall. Let me tell you, I thought the world was over for me. Anyone who's lost their job knows what I mean. I'd been on TV shows that weren't picked up after a season or two. Or they were canceled. But those were different. I was playing a character. I recited someone else's lines. On *Valerie's*

Home Cooking, it wasn't a script or just a job—it was *me*. My heart. My history. My life wrapped up in recipes and love and laughter.

I spent seven years and fourteen seasons in the kitchen, sharing family favorites with viewers and serving them to my parents, my son, close friends, and colleagues. I told personal stories, revealed secrets, made fun of myself when I flubbed something, and proudly showed off my culinary successes. In the beginning, it was a leap of faith. I didn't quite know what I was doing. It was a fake-it-till-you-make-it situation. Then I got pretty good at it. Kind of the story of my life.

It was my life. It earned two Emmy Awards and eight total nominations. It connected me to generations of women in my family who had turned their kitchens into the beating hearts of family life. I know that for the most part, acting on a TV show isn't comparable to the jobs most people do, but I think my approach to *Valerie's Home Cooking* was similar to how some people live their career and aspire to be really good at it. I worked hard. I took the work home with me. I surrounded myself with cookbooks and food-oriented magazines. Dinner parties were more like test kitchens. It wasn't just professional. It was personal.

I took it hard when word came that the network wasn't picking it up. Something was said about cost-cutting, but no concrete explanation was given. My ratings were good and the show brought in more money than it cost. The bottom line? I was fired. Just . . . done. I suffered the way everyone does who has been let go, laid off, downsized, or canned. First came shock, then anger, and then sadness.

I tried to rationalize the network's decision. I told myself that it wasn't personal. The man who bought the network had debt to pay for investments in other entities. Everything was being cut back.

It was business. "But I thought they liked me," I whimpered. It felt like a rejection of me, of a partnership I'd built with this network. They didn't want to be married anymore, not even friends. I was already going through a divorce; I didn't think I could survive another one. My anger returned ("I guess you're telling me that I added no value to your network . . . well, #*%$ you!"), followed by confusion and anxiety about what might be next.

I posted a thank-you to fans: "It has been one of the huge joys in my life to bring you this sweet little show."

I walked into my backyard and became one of those people who talks out loud to the universe. "Why are you kicking a girl when she's down?" The universe answered back, as it usually does—with a phone call. I had a long talk with one of my closest girlfriends. The gist of what she said is this: *Your life isn't over. No one said the words* malignant *or* inoperable *or* terminal. *You're a good person. You're surrounded by love. You'll get another job. You'll do something else.*

* * *

The last time I threw myself across my bed the way I did later that day was when I was seventeen years old and my boyfriend broke up with me. My heart was shattered. I was on a top-rated TV series watched by twenty million people or more each week, yet I thought my life was done. "You'll get over it," my mom said. "You'll survive." I didn't feel like it. But all was not lost. A few weeks later the phone rang. A cute guy asked me out to dinner. I didn't say, "Sorry, my life is over." I said, "Great, what time?"

I don't know how my mom continued on after losing my brother when he was only seventeen months old. I thought only of the pain, the grief, the inability to fix such a grave and incomprehensible occurrence. A child's death—my God. Wouldn't life just stop? I didn't understand the resilience of the human heart, the way our DNA is programmed to go on, to wail beneath the empathetic moon and heal in the warmth of the sun. Neither did I give my mom enough credit when I was younger. I gingerly broached the subject toward the end of her life, when we were finally able to have meaningful conversations. My eyes did most of the asking when I said, "What about Mark?" "It was tragic," she said. "But I had a family. I wanted more children. I was already pregnant with you. You find a way forward or . . . I guess you don't." I've miscarried, and I have friends who have endured the same painful event, and whose children have also lost pregnancies. "You'll try again," we tell them. People put their family pets down. "Sending prayers," we say. "And get another dog when you're ready." Others have lost spouses to illness and we say, "I don't know what to tell you other than you have to put one foot in front of the other. Eventually, it will hurt less." More recently, everybody I know seems to know someone whose home burned in the LA fires. "You'll rebuild."

It sounds cavalier and callous. And it feels cavalier and callous. Sadly, this stuff happens. All. The. Time. We fall in so many different ways. We have even more ways of encouraging each other to get back up. Hang in there. Go for it. Keep pushing. You can do it. Get back in the saddle. I've had a quote taped to my computer for what feels like forever: "Life doesn't put things in front of you that you are unable to handle." All of this is well intentioned, but sometimes it doesn't help as much as when someone says, "Do you need to cry?" "I'm here for you." Or "I know it's hard. What do you need? How can I help?"

I thought about all the times I'd gotten back up before. All the times I'd wiped out skiing in Park City, only to brush off the snow and race down the mountain again. All the times I'd lost acting jobs, faced rejections, felt like I was falling apart—only to realize, later, that I was just making room for something new.

So, I let myself feel it. The loss, the uncertainty, the frustration. I let myself cry. I let myself grieve. And then I started moving again. First on automatic pilot, then with intention. I reminded myself that I had been feeling good about myself before I got the pink slip. Things hadn't been perfect, but I didn't want to lose that momentum. I didn't know what would come next, but I knew I had to keep showing up for my life. I wrote a book. Then I wrote a cookbook. Then I wrote a big fat check to my ex. I was free in every possible way. I was also going broke.

This was a moment unlike any I had experienced in my life. I was all alone, on my own, without a safety net. Or so I thought, so I felt. Both of my parents were gone. I had two exes—one passed away, the other sent away. My son had moved out of the house long ago and was pursuing his own life. Happily married and with a career in music taking off. My brothers resided in other states. I was unemployed and dipping into savings. I did have family and friends, but for all practical purposes, I was flying solo.

I kept waiting for the crash, the fall that I knew was coming as sure as I knew I would wipe out sooner or later when I used to ski the treacherous black diamond runs. But you know what's worse than falling? Not getting back up. Not believing that there's something on the other side of the fall that's worth reaching for. I thought about people who had faced real shit: Christopher Reeve saying the horse-riding accident that left him paralyzed made him more appreciative of life. Poet Andrea Gibson writing "How the Worst Day of My Life Became My Best" after their cancer diagnosis. If they could deal with the immensity of that, I could get through my iota of shit. Buck up, buttercup. So I kept believing. I took my daily walks. My Dry January became a Dry Spring. I went to Pilates. I kept in touch with friends. And I traveled to New York to promote the publication of my cookbook.

I just kept going—and something unexpected happened. I stayed on my skis. I even added a little speed to my run. So what if I fell again. I'd spent decades falling. Though I might not have felt as steady on my feet physically as I once did, I was getting more solid than ever on the inside. Not impervious to pain but more grounded, centered, and wiser. I had sixty-plus years of experience to temper the uncertainty that too often tripped me up in my thirties, forties, and fifties. I was strong. I was resilient.

You know how you hear older people say something isn't worth falling apart over? I was that older person telling myself things weren't worth falling apart over.

* * *

When I started promoting my cookbook in New York, one of my first stops was *The Drew Barrymore Show*. Though I had never met Drew in person, I had an immediate connection with her as soon as I walked onto the set. I sensed a kindred soul, a truth seeker and a truth teller, someone who'd been through the entire wash cycle more than a few times. She seemed to have a quiet pride of the colors that still shone bright and didn't mind those that had faded. It was like both of us had embraced comedian Flip Wilson's old drag queen Geraldine's attitude: "What you see is what you get!"

I've known her cohost Ross Mathews for years and always adored him. How can you not love someone who radiates joy, humor, and gratitude the way he does? Who turns everything that makes him unique into a celebration? Everyone who works behind the scenes reflects their positivity. So it felt comfortable to sit across from them that day. Better still, I felt like they clicked with me. We had a great couple of segments and not long after, I put out feelers that I would love to be a part of their show in any way they would have me. I was invited to join the show for its fifth season as part of "Drew's Crew."

"We love you," they said. What did they want me to do? "Be you. Just be Valerie."

I was stunned in the best possible way. I was still smarting from being canned by the Food Network, but then I heard that these kind, clever people whose goal was to inject goodness into the world every day wanted me—not a character but *me*, my authentic, loud, unfiltered, emotional, honest, imperfect self—to join their team. Cue the tears. Pass the tissues. Send a text to God: Thank you.

Midway through my first year on the show, Drew's show felt as close to a home as I've ever felt on a set. I think all people want to feel this way, welcomed and encouraged to be themselves, to be valued for who they are. There's an ease, a calmness, an equanimity, a chemistry when you feel like you belong. Brené Brown talks about the difference between belonging and fitting in. The former is being accepted for who you are; the latter is about changing to be part of a group. It's like a puzzle piece when you don't have to force the fit. It just slides into the picture.

None of which means more falls aren't ahead. They most assuredly are. In fact, the proof is on my arm. While emceeing a new series for the Game Show Network, I walked onto the set one morning and went over to introduce myself to a cameraman I hadn't met yet. The set was dark, and I clumsily tripped on the corner of the stage. The sharp edge put a six-inch shallow gash on my forearm. I felt it throbbing, but I wasn't sure what it looked like under my long-sleeved sweater until we finished the first show and I was back in my dressing room, changing clothes for the second show. My arm was swollen, bruised a dark purple and bright pink color, and covered with a thin coat of dried blood. I was advised to go to the ER, but I wasn't going to shut down production.

"Are you sure you're all right?" a producer asked.

"This is nothing," I said, wiping the blood off my arm.

This is what we do. We fall. We curse. We laugh at ourselves. Sometimes we cry. And then we rise—sometimes with a little scar to remind us of our resiliency.

if i could talk to my animals

(and if they could talk to me)

I want to build and wear down a path to happiness and let the path to sadness grow weeds.

JOURNAL ENTRY, APRIL 2024

I AM A pet person. That means my fallback position is patience. It also means my go-to position is love. Pet people all share one common characteristic besides the obvious: We have a soft, gooey center. When the going gets rough, we cuddle with our pets. When no human understands what we're going through, we tell our animals everything and they get it. When things are good, we basically French kiss them.* It's gross. It's love.

I wish I could see myself the way my pets see me. They surely notice my flaws, but they don't let those define me the way I have for so much of my life. I think this is true for most people's pets. They see the whole picture—the good, the messy, the vulnerable, the potential. Everything that makes us human. They don't see me as fat or thin, grouchy or cheerful, too much or not enough. They don't judge. They don't try to change me. They leave that to me.

They love me unconditionally as I am and how I am. They let me fail, grow, and keep trying. "You're my person no matter what," they say.

And even though I know the difference between people and animals, I say it back: "You're my person, too."

And when they leave us? Forget about it. With me, we're talking about a once-in-a-generation flood of tears. I was thinking about this the day after my cat Nelson died. My eyes were swollen from crying. Nelson was a gorgeous buff tabby who I fostered after my other cat Dexter passed in 2013. Dexter was a stunning Abyssinian and the love of my life. He was the last cat I ever purchased at a pet store, which I didn't realize then but know now that you should never do. But it was a moment of instant attraction. I turned, he was looking at me, and shazam, it was a love match.

---

* I'm exaggerating of course, and I'm talking about dogs in this specific instance. Cats are more particular about making out. Some are fine with it. Some prefer more formal European air kisses. I prefer giving all of them multiple forehead and neck kisses until they pull away.

Dexter, to me, was part dog and part psychic in a cat's body. In other words, he was an elevated soul. He knew me like nobody else. That look he gave me in the pet store turned into a look that might say, "Really, Val?" or "We're going to get through this" or "When was the last time you called your mom?" or "Don't feel bad, eat the licorice." We went through everything together. If there is reincarnation, which I believe there is, the two of us were involved in some way in a previous life and will likely meet up again.

When Dexter died, I was working on *Hot in Cleveland*, and I was totally gutted by the loss. A few months later, I was telling a woman on the crew that I wanted to get a new cat, but I had Deedee at home, another older cat, and she wasn't doing well. I didn't want to upset her. "You're not ready," she said. "Maybe you should foster instead." I hadn't heard about fostering animals at that time. But the concept, as she explained it, made sense. You bring a kitten into your house from the shelter, where they're kept in cages, and they become socialized, increasing their chance of being adopted.

I was in. I knew a few people who could've benefited from that kind of socializing. Actually, stray and abandoned animals aside, shouldn't we be fostering each other in some way? Gradual exposure to new places, animals, and other humans in a loving and safe environment. It's a no-brainer. Don't get me started. Kittens were fun. I came home from the shelter with two adorable fluffballs, Nelson and his sister. Soon I found a home for Nelson's sister: One of the wardrobe assistants took her. A sweet woman who assisted in craft service took Nelson, but she called the next day, upset, saying she couldn't keep him because she got a job out of town that was going to keep her away for more than a month.

So I welcomed Nelson back home. He didn't have a name yet.

Betty White actually came up with his name. I was telling her that I had decided to keep this cute little foster kitten but didn't know what to name him. "Oh, I always wanted a cat named Nelson Eddy," she said with emphatic sweetness before explaining that Eddy was an actor and wonderful singer in musicals in the 1930s and '40s. "Name him Nelson." I had a soft spot for him from the beginning because he looked like Edgar, a cat that Ed and I had had when we were together. I adored Edgar.

Fun fact: Edgar was curled up in Ed's lap when he wrote "Jump."

Nelson grew up to be a good-looking charmer, more like a camp counselor. He cuddled with all the new cats I brought home. I bragged about socializing kitties from the shelter, but he actually did the work acclimating all of them. I relied on him for years without fully considering how much I take for granted the joy I get from him and the others—the way Batman jumps up on the bed every night after I get in and burrows close to, if not directly on top of, me; Tig's trills at the top of the stairs every morning when I come out of my bedroom; and Henry's romance with my daughter-in-law, Draia.

Seriously, Henry is absolutely gaga over Draia. I am aware that dogs and cats can be attracted to certain people, but they aren't supposed to have feelings the way that humans do. I flat out disagree and offer as proof Henry's feelings for her. It's like a schoolboy's crush, the kind that has him bumping into walls and unable to focus on anything else. He senses when she drives up and knows it's her before she even opens the door. He's Robert Redford gazing at Barbra Streisand in *The Way We Were*—Hubbell in love with Katie. He sits beside Draia and doesn't move. He literally shivers when she touches him. Tell me that's not love.

* * *

Here's something I wonder about all the time: Why is it so much easier to say "I love you" to my dog, Luna, or one of my cats than it is to say it to another human being? Why is love so much easier to find—and give—to a pet than to a person? Why do I feel more comfortable confiding in my animals than in my closest friends, or even my therapist? Is this true for most people? Am I the only weirdo out here? Is it because I don't want to be seen as too needy? Or is it as simple as wanting to be heard—or loved unconditionally without fear of it being pulled away or judged?

I've been surrounded by pets since I was a kid. My mom had a basset hound she absolutely adored. She was a cat lover, too, but I know she had a soft spot for Barney. So did I. Barney had this way of turning his head and looking at you like he was saying, "Okay, I'm ready for a hug," and I had no choice but to oblige.

Then there was our Dalmatian, Sherman. Gorgeous—and he knew it. But in a shy, almost catlike way.

I love you, Sherman. Do you love me?

Could you rub my stomach while I think about it?

Before Wolfie came along, I would take long hikes with Shermie. It would help me clear my head when Ed and I were having rough patches. Sherm and I went so far up a canyon one day and his panting was so labored I thought I had broken him. He looked at me like I was crazy. "Girl, you have got to stop," his eyes clearly said. "Are you running away from something? This ain't normal. This is supposed to be a leisurely walk. We are not training for an Ironman."

We took much shorter walks from then on, and I found a therapist to talk it out with instead of taking the chance of killing my dog on the trail. He would also join me outside as I puttered in what I called my garden, though in reality it was a bunch of bricked planters surrounding our pool. Later that night, after a long day of planting flowers, I would look outside from the kitchen window and see a few flowers pulled out and deeper dirt holes dug in their place. Payback for the long hikes? Only Sherman knows.

My current dog, Luna, is . . . well, I couldn't have asked for a better companion. Patient, selfless, intuitive—she's a listener. She's never once brought up the baggage she carried before I rescued her. She gets spooked around some men,* but other than that, the moment she came home with us, she let most of it go and decided life at chez Bertinelli was the good life. I've spent my whole adult life trying to let go of baggage. Why can't I be more like her?

She likes the music I play, the shows I watch, and living with a clowder of cats. Every day, she thanks me with those soulful eyes that always seem to be saying one of three things: "Wanna go for a walk?" "Feel like talking about it?" Or "Is it time for a treat?"

That's the brilliance of dogs. They live in the moment, without judgment, forgiving to a fault, happy for life's simple pleasures. A squirrel to chase, a doorbell ringing, an ear rub, a toy to chew on—they're in heaven. They move on quickly from irritations, and they ask for help when they need it. Ever seen a dog that's stepped on a thorn or been stung by a bee? Then you *know*.

Cats, on the other hand, are more like me when they're not feeling well. Quiet, withdrawn, sipping water, refusing food. *Just leave me alone, don't ask how I'm doing. I'll let you know when I'm better.* If I'm feeling vulnerable, I reach for a cat and hold it close. Why not my dog, who'd kill for me? It's about my cats' inner strength and emotional

---

* I mean, some men spook me, too, so who am I to judge my dog?

intelligence. They'll brood with me. We'll explore our feelings, rerun conversations, and purr together till I'm more settled. It is said that a cat purring on your chest can reduce stress and lower blood pressure. From experience, I know this to be true.

If I'm feeling low, it's Luna time. She puts her cold nose on my cheek and basically quotes Winnie-the-Pooh from the movie *Sing a Song with Pooh Bear*, when he says in his gentle way, "A day spent with you is my favorite day. So today is my new favorite day." I mean . . . instant boost.

We all know cats aren't model citizens. If they were, I would not have rolls of plastic cat spikes covering my kitchen counter. And I wouldn't have suffered a broken foot because one was stuck in the bathroom sink! I'm also convinced that if any of mine could speak—Batman, Henry, or one of the others—they'd all be threatening poor Yelp reviews: *Feed me. Why aren't you feeding me more? My God, lady, you get whatever you want whenever you want. You're three minutes and forty-two seconds late with our wet food—we can't live on dry food alone, woman! Would it kill you to be less stingy with the treats?* And honestly, I can only imagine what else they've been itching to get off their chests.

Do we need six bags of Trader Joe's fruit-flavored licorice twists in the pantry?

Why are you still paying for a landline when everybody calls on your cell?

How many pairs of shoes does one human need? Or are you opening up a museum?

Why are you skipping Pilates this week? What's the excuse now?

Why do you blame all of us for peeing around the house when everyone knows it's Batman marking territory?

Brutal, right? But these animals spend every day of their lives observing me.* They know me better than I know me. They watch me in the morning. They're in the bathroom when I'm showering. They study me while I'm in my closet, figuring out what I am going to wear that day. They listen to me talk on the phone. They take cover when I blast my son's new album and dance around the house. They stare at me when I cook. They watch what I watch on TV and go to bed when I do—I think. And I am absolutely sure they talk about me when I'm not around.

What was with her hair today? Show of paws—who liked the bangs?

She cut them herself. Again. Something must be up.

Forget her hair, what was with her second marriage?

Now, don't be catty.

You're really going there?

Why can't she meet a good guy? Or the right guy? Only dogs.

Sorry, Luna.

Did you get a whiff of the vongole she made the other night? The butter? The sausage? Mmmm. I'd marry her, but I've been living with her for ten years. Why change a good thing?

She's late for our dinner again. It's way past four thirty.

I love her, though.

She's too hard on herself.

She was crying in bed again after getting off the phone.

She cries easily.

I'm going to jump in her lap when she comes home.

I'm going to jump in her lap when she's trying to finish the crossword.

I'm going to cuddle extra close tonight at bedtime.

---

* Perhaps another reason the cats often look bored.

While you do that, I'm going to jump up on the kitchen counter and see what food she has up there.

I'm going to go rub up against her Uggs and think about all the ways I love her.

Uh-oh, who peed in the laundry room? Batman? Where's Batman?

* * *

Batman is the bane of my existence, and I couldn't live without him, which he seems to know. He went missing one day. A whole posse of family and friends came over to help look for him. We covered every inch of the house and the front and back yards. Finally, after eight hours (yes, eight hours—I counted) of searching, we found him lounging under a bush not twenty feet from the back door. He had watched the entire drama unfold. Was he playing? Was it a cry for attention? Was he on the prowl? Or was he protecting me?

I've come to think that he *was* protecting me. He knew I needed company. I'd been spending too much time alone, brooding, overthinking, avoiding. I think he turned himself into a service animal—not that animals aren't always serving us merely by their presence—and set up a situation where he knew I needed my friends and family around me and the hugs that everyone gave me following his return. I felt relieved. My freak-out was understood. I was loved.

And Batman? After I sobbed, holding him tight until he was wet with my tears, he jumped off my lap and ate his dinner with total indifference to the commotion he'd caused.

Later, we got into bed together as always—me first, then he jumped up and cozied himself on my chest so that he was looking directly into my eyes. "Really, Batman?" I asked. "Was all that necessary?" He meowed loudly at me, crawled to my side, and cuddled in the crook of my arm, where he started purring and fell fast asleep.

These are difficult times personally and collectively. Uncertainty hangs in the air like dark clouds blocking the warmth of the sun. Not knowing drives everyone crazy. This is when I rely on my animals. They seem to know it, too. The cats loll in bed with me. Henry will jump on my lap or Luna will rest her chin on my leg. We'll look at each other for a while. I'll absorb their strength and practical sensibility, their calm.

Take it day by day, moment by moment. Don't catastrophize. They're right. "We're going to get through it," I'll say, as if I came up with that myself. "We're going to be okay."

I haven't mentioned Bubba and Beau yet. They were my parents' cats. After my mom died, I brought them to LA from Arizona so they could live with me. They often remind me of my parents in some way, as if my mom and dad are still with me, which they are. That's the lesson I've learned from grieving their loss or any other loss. People go away physically, but the love remains. Bubba and Beau always seem to give me the right amount of affection when I need it.*

My friend's daughter is married with a one-year-old son and, until recently, a seventeen-year-old dog named Banksy. Banksy was a medium-size rescue, a white-haired terrier-chihuahua mix. She had long legs and the presence of a supermodel, though if you weren't part of her immediate family, she turned into John Wick. I know

---

* Bubba has turned into Wolfie's cat. As soon as Wolfie comes over, he takes off his shoes and Bubba rubs them and lies on them. It's become a thing between them. Now every time Wolfie is about to go on tour, he comes over to get a little Bubba rub on his shoes. Beau has always been the shiest, and Wolfie is the only one who can bring him out of wherever he's hiding. He drools with happiness with what we call "Beau's tunnel time with Wolfie."

from firsthand experience. Also, she hated little kids until my friend's daughter had her own son. From day one, she was by his side, part mom, part secret service agent.

How do dogs know? It's beautiful and mind-boggling, but they know. By then, however, Banksy's health was declining, and within six months or so she was succumbing to the frailties of old age. Her last morning was spent sitting next to the baby while he played around her, one life beginning, the other diminished from dementia, blindness, and other bodily failures. The vet said the end was the compassionate thing to do.

My reason for mentioning all this is because a couple of weeks later my friend's daughter visited the same chiropractor–energy healer whom I occasionally see. As Dr. Tracy worked on her neck and hip, she sensed a sadness in her body and asked if anything had happened recently to cause it. She mentioned having put her dog down. Dr. Tracy did her thing, whatever that is, and said, "Banksy wants you to know that she wasn't ready to go, but she understands why you thought it was time. She is okay with the decision, and she is fine. She's still here. You can't see her anymore, but your son can. She's not his guardian angel, but she's still with him—and will be for a while."

Soon after that her baby said his first word: *doggie*.

* * *

I think God created dogs to remind us of the best, most loving versions of ourselves. Cats are a more complicated story, almost a test. They insist we prove ourselves before they reveal the intimacies of their devotion. Both teach us about our responsibility to each other. We have to provide food, shelter, and care. I'm constantly asking, "How're you doing? What do you need?"

I do now talk to my animals. Luna is the first being I say good morning to. Tigger and I have our morning love fest at the top of the stairs. One day, as I cooed "You're such a handsome boy" and "Hello, beautiful girl, did you have a good day?" I wondered why I didn't talk to myself the way I did to my pets, with kindness, tolerance, and forgiveness. Why hadn't I realized this earlier, say, fifty years earlier? How different I might have treated myself if I had looked in the mirror and said things like, "You are so smart," "Who has the cutest little belly?," and "I love you."*

We wonder what really matters. Our pets teach us. Companionship. Love. The gift of being here, life itself. I spent last New Year's Eve at the vet with Nelson. One, two, and then two and a half hours went by. Finally, I was told Nelson wasn't stable enough to go home. His heart was enlarged and he needed help breathing.

I walked outside with an empty carrier. The vet's office was next door to a restaurant where people were celebrating New Year's. I heard them counting down the seconds: five, four, three, two, one, *Happy New Year!* I sat in my car and cried. Three days later I brought Nelson home. For the next six weeks I flew back and forth to New York nearly every week for work. One weekend I was going to stay over to minimize the travel and have fun, but plans changed at the last minute and I went home. I even got a flight a day earlier than I first booked. I thought, "Why wait?"

If there's a higher power, she had swept me up in her arms because, in retrospect, that whole sequence of events seems predetermined. I got home and saw that Nelson wasn't doing well. He could barely lift

---

* I also know we say things like "Don't eat that—that's garbage," "Be nice, no growling," "Don't even think about peeing there while I'm out," and "Please! I'm begging, stay off the counters."

his head. I left my luggage by the door and took him to the emergency vet. The vet turned to me after examining him and I instantly knew the diagnosis. "It's not good, is it?" I asked. She just shook her head.

I didn't bother to ask how much time we had. I'd been through this before with people and animals I loved as much as I could possibly love. Time was immaterial. That's the lesson in these events. At the end, you better have done all the living you intended to do and said all the things you needed to say because there is no more time. The vet sat down next to me. The same vet who saw him on New Year's Eve. "You can take him home and have a vet come to the house like you did with Dexter. Or we can do it here."

I didn't hear her at first. I was lost in thought, remembering when I first brought Nelson home and this last car ride we had just taken together. His breaths were labored. Mine were wet with tears. He stared at me, seeing me the way I hope to see myself one day, seeing us together, and knowing whatever there was to know about what was next. "Thank you," he seemed to say.

I told the vet there was no point in putting off the inevitable. I scooped Nelson up in my arms and held him tightly. He was as comfortable as he was ever going to be. She took him back and put an IV in him, then gave him back to me. She told me to take as long as I wanted. I don't know if I held him for five minutes or two hours. We melded into each other, he nuzzled into my neck, and I said over and over the only thing that mattered: "I love you I love you I love you I love you I love you I love you I love you I love—"

Finally, I was interrupted by a gentle knock on the door. I looked up at the vet, she looked at me with shared pain, and I simply nodded.

"Tell me that I'm doing the right thing," I said.

"You're doing the right thing."

getting naked

I am here to learn and to love.

JOURNAL ENTRY, MARCH 2025

ONE NIGHT LAST summer I went skinny-dipping. Should I have been doing that at my age? I didn't think about age appropriateness or right or wrong. I just did it—and no one was more surprised than me.

It was a warm and velvety evening in the Valley. I was between jobs, as we actors say, and still licking my wounds after my divorce. My bank account felt about as low as my spirit, so these were not my easiest days. I'd been pacing around the house muttering to myself: "What am I supposed to be learning in all of this? What is the lesson?! How is this fair? How much did I have to pay to be free?"

Then the anger and frustration eased. "Whatever," I said to myself. The cost was worth every penny. What's the line from that Kris Kristofferson and Janis Joplin song? "Freedom's just another word for nothin' left to lose." It bought me relief. The fighting and haggling ended. I was free.

After a light dinner, I wasn't ready for TV or sleep. I didn't feel like the former and it was too early for the latter, even for me. I stepped outside to breathe in the summer night. No alcohol was involved—just a cocktail of gratitude, orange blossoms, and roses from my garden. The moon hung low and golden, like a smile or a wink from the universe. I saw an owl's silhouette on a top tree branch.

"Who?"

"Me."

"Who?"

"I told you." I giggled. "It's me."

It all felt delicious and alive—and the next thing I knew, I was peeling off my clothes and diving into my pool, buckass naked as the day I was born.

I swam a few slow laps. Got used to the water—and used to being naked outside. All of Los Angeles could see me if they knew the right perch and had a pair of high-powered binoculars handy. A Southwest Airlines jet taking off from Hollywood Burbank Airport flew overhead. I waved. The security cameras around my yard? I waved to them, too. Why not?

I felt naughty in the best way—like a cosmic reminder: "Hey, girl, you're alive! Enjoy it!" I kicked off the wall and swam. The feeling was wonderful. The water held me like a secret. I was buoyant. Light. Weightless.

Weightless!

I understood why dolphins leap out of the water. They're happy! I couldn't remember the last time I had gone skinny-dipping, if ever. When I was younger? No, I couldn't recall any swims au naturel. Even then, I was self-conscious about a body that I had no business being self-conscious about. But not tonight! Tonight, I flippered through the water and felt . . . good. My limbs were strong, my body capable, my skin unjudged. No tugging at my swimsuit, no concerns about whether it was flattering. I wasn't wearing a stitch of clothing and I fit perfectly in my skin.

What a revelation. To be comfortable in my own skin.

It was a shift. Just weeks earlier, I'd been at a dinner party with friends when I noticed my arms. To be more precise, I noticed the loose skin on my forearms and upper arms had changed. I cut into a piece of flank steak and there it was: a jiggle. I cut another piece, this time staring straight at it. I was stunned. A decade earlier my arms had been well toned. Three years ago they were still toned. Only five minutes ago they were still toned, or so I had thought.

"What the fudge?" I said aloud.

"What?" my friends asked.

"My arms. Look."

"What about them?"

"Look at that skin." I flicked it. It wasn't flab. I wasn't out of shape. It was . . . gravity. I sneered.

They laughed. I did, too. I mean, gravity? The thing that keeps everything grounded—cars, homes, pets, football stadiums, the water in the oceans, the air we breathe? Without it, we would disappear, too. But saying gravity was having that effect on my arms was ridiculous. Age and genetics were the real culprits.

"Is this the end of tank tops and short sleeves?" I asked.

Back home, I googled the hell out of it and found there are names for this anatomical condition—bat wings or bingo wings.* One person called them "choir teacher arms." Another person called them "mah sisters." I loved that one. I also found an official medical term: upper arm ptosis. And of course, there is a plastic surgery procedure for this—an arm lift.

I didn't want to fix anything. I started calling them mah sisters. They are part of me, evidence of the change that comes with age, change I can't control or stop even if I wanted to, which I don't. I'm happy with my age. My arms work fine. I use them every day. They brush my teeth, make my coffee, feed my pets, steer my car, cut the flowers I put into vases, make my meals, hug my kid and his wife. They're not saggy. They're seasoned.

Bless you, *mah sisters*.

---

* Nothing quite as fun for what they call what was happening to my forearms; that is simply called forearm sagging.

* * *

I got out of the pool and dried off. I felt good standing in the warm air, under the stars, connected to the universe, me wearing nothing but me. *Hello, my body.* I was in no rush to cover myself or go back inside. How often had I craved a moment like this? To feel joy. To feel good. To appreciate my body and myself in this way, undressed and unconcerned. I'd said it so many times, I almost feared being numb to the experience if it ever happened. Yet here it was, joy, a lightness of being, an appreciation of being alive, the night air kissing my skin. I was slow dancing the moment. When was the last time I had felt this way? This good?

I breathed it in. Really breathed. The kind of breathing you do when you're trying to hold on to a feeling so it doesn't float away.* I looked up to face the night sky, closed my eyes, and whispered, "Thank you."

Eventually, I draped my towel over a chair, picked up my clothes, and wandered toward the house. I slipped on pj's and brushed my teeth. In the mirror, I saw someone I'd spent decades hating. But why? Why had I judged her so harshly?

I once gave a keynote address at a women's conference in Arizona a few months after I had dieted myself into a bikini for my job as a spokesperson for Jenny Craig. The weight loss and media attention brought much admiration for "still looking hot" as I turned fifty years old. The audience applauded when I shared the details of my struggle with weight and body image and the willpower it took to shed

---

* Suddenly, I was a yogi—and I don't do yoga.

the pounds. I showed a lot of skin and revealed a herculean ability to starve myself. But really, I was *starving*—myself and my soul.

I look back now and cringe when I think about being part of the obsessed diet culture and industry. I probably did more harm than good. I was taught, in many ways, from when I was a young girl, that what I weighed meant something. It was either good or bad depending. And what it means to be "healthy" changes with the wind. I'm still annoyed that the bikini I wore was a size L. A large! I weighed 122 pounds and am five feet, four inches tall. How does that equate to a large? Oh, for Christ's sake, I can't believe I am still litigating this nonsense to myself. Size really has become such a mind game. It's supposed to simply be a number or letter to divide garments to help you find a pair of pants online or in a store, not screw with your sense of self-worth.

At the conference, I told the audience that the real work was keeping the weight off. What I should've said is the real work was healing what made me hate myself in the first place. Taking care of the weight that I carried on my shoulders, the weight that made me heavy inside. And I hadn't done that. Not then.

I would get on the scale every morning, but I wouldn't look at my reflection. I avoided the mirror like it was Bloody Mary—like the legend: Say her name five times in the mirror and her ghost appears to scare the bejeezus out of you. What I feared wasn't my body—it was seeing what was behind my eyes.

* * *

A woman came up to me in the airport recently. "You're too skinny," she said. Others have echoed that. "Don't lose any more weight.

You're too thin." I weighed myself this morning. I was 141 pounds. I wear size 10 jeans. How is that too skinny? And how is it anyone's business? I know, people care—and I appreciate that. It's an amazing perk in my life. To be connected to strangers, to be seen, to have people care about you. Who doesn't want that? But that kind of comment used to spin me out. Now I didn't know how to respond. It called for a conversation that neither of us probably had time for while hurrying across the airport terminal. I do think we all need to get a lot less comfortable commenting on people's bodies. I felt good the way I was. I wasn't the smallest or largest I've ever been. I was just existing in my body without judgment. I felt healthy.

Feeling this way was something I was getting used to after so many years of hating on my body. I didn't expect to feel this way in my sixties.

Hello, mah sisters!

It was about time. After my second marriage ended, something had to give or else I was going to end up an unhappy old lady—and what was the point of that? We are given choices all through life, and I had to make one: keep obsessing about my weight and body and punishing myself with food and alcohol, or face the hard truths that were at the root of my self-hate, my shame, and low self-esteem. I should add the word *finally*—as in finally face those hard truths I knew were inside me.

Let me back up a bit. See, once I gave up looking for a magic number on the scale, once I quit thinking of food as good and bad, and settled into a place that felt healthy and proved sustainable, I thought I was done with my healing journey. Finished with the work. Therapy, retreats, tears on national TV as I told my story, oversharing on

Instagram—check, check, check. I did it all. My weight was back to stable. Physically, I had few complaints that didn't have to do with the common creaks of being in my mid-sixties. Hallelujah. I had planted a flag atop my personal Everest.

But my mental health was another story—one I had purposely avoided telling myself. It was the story behind my eyes, the reason I avoided my reflection. I still had doors in my past marked "No Entrance." Deep down, I knew this about myself. And maybe my weight was simply more information. Another symptom of something deeper that needed to be looked at. I think this is something many of us have in common. We carry around these wounds, traumas we keep private, things we try to forget ever happened. But we know better. In our quietest, most vulnerable moments, we go back to them. Over and over again.

Years pass. We grow up. And they're still with us. We hear the hurt. We feel the assault. We know the hold it has over us, the sway it has over our self-esteem, the way it keeps our emotional lives on rinse and repeat. Hey, it took me over sixty years to go skinny-dipping! But I knew that was only the start. Yes, I took my clothes off, but . . . I wasn't really getting naked.

It's one thing to let the world see your private parts. It's another to look at your most private parts yourself, what you and only you can see. To me, getting naked means walking into those shadows, turning on the light, acknowledging the thing that happened, confronting it, understanding it, talking to it, owning it, taking away its power, ending the cycle of low self-esteem and shame.

For me, this revelation was only the start. I knew where it was eventually going to take me. It was only a matter of courage, resolve, and time.

* * *

One day, while returning from Pilates class—a three-mile walk to my house—I passed a storefront psychic. The door was open and a woman leaned against the side of the doorframe. I noticed her place was decorated with hanging crystals, posters of Tarot cards, a couple of chairs, and a small table between them. But it was the psychic lady who caught my attention. I had walked past this storefront at least a hundred times previously without ever seeing anyone there. I smiled at her and kept going.

"Hello!" she called out after I walked past.

I turned around. She had stepped beyond the door and was standing out front, looking at me. She was short, with dark hair, and dressed in a long-sleeved boatneck T-shirt and baggy stone-washed jeans. Her sleeves were pushed up.

"Oh. Hi."

"Are you troubled?" she said. "You look sad."

Her comment startled me. She wasn't wrong. My life was in flux. I had a lot of uncertainty. It was yet another transition for me. I was trying to make sense of things and move on but also bogged down by questions I couldn't seem to answer. Why had my marriage ended? Why had I said "I do" in the first place? I wanted to believe I was a fundamentally good person. I treated others with kindness. I had my moods, like anyone, but friends, family, and animals I treated with care. I was a do-unto-others gal. Why did my life feel like such an emotional struggle? What was wrong with me?

Maybe nothing that major. Today I felt good! I felt strong in Pilates. I'd had some fun gossip time with my friend Jo and Grace, our instructor. I thought I was on an upswing. But I often forget my face shows everything. Especially the things I'm trying to forget or push aside.

"Do you want to come in?" the psychic asked.

I declined. But her words stuck. *Sad*. That's what my eyes had been saying even when my body felt good. My eyes always told the truth. That's why I love certain photos—when I look really happy, relaxed happy. Not deer-in-the-headlights-look-at-me-acting happy, but happy. I can see it in my eyes.

Betty White had eyes that lit up a room. All her wisdom, humor, and intelligence were apparent when you looked into her baby blues. She had a special aura, and it was most visible in her eyes. After we began working together on *Hot in Cleveland*, I saw the side of her that was all knowing. She took in everything that was going on. She rarely made other people's business her own, but her eyes always gave away whether she approved or disapproved.

My girlfriends are the same way. Norman Lear, too. He understood so much, and it was all in his eyes. He looked at you with love. Ed's eyes were soulful and soft. They were kind and occasionally melancholic. I thought I could stare into them forever. And then a couple's therapist we were seeing told us to do just that. To sit close and stare directly into each other's eyes for ten minutes without looking away.

Doing that for even one minute was extremely uncomfortable. It was intense and terrifying. But we held it. And then it was transcendent. We experienced a deeply powerful, soulful connection. I saw the truth about Ed and me. I experienced our secrets. We might have had our troubles, but there was a reason we were together. The revelation was magical. But you can't build a life on fleeting magic.

GETTING NAKED

* * *

These days I start some mornings not by getting on the scale but instead stepping in front of the mirror and looking directly into my eyes the way Ed and I did. Quiet, calm, still, contemplative, inquisitive, open, nonjudgmental, compassionate, loving. I look. I search. I take full, deep, nourishing breaths. I listen to my heartbeat. I come into focus. There is no fat or thin, good or bad. Instead, I see layers of me. At first, I saw my mother, as relatives had always remarked when they saw me when I was younger. She was curvy and voluptuous. Then I started to also see my nonnie, Angelina. Her beautiful hands, her strong, aging body.

Then, gradually, I saw . . . me. Complicated. Understanding. Forgiving. Stubborn. Goofy. Loyal. I scrunched up my face. I smiled. My eyes were open, inviting, apologetic. How could I have ever hated my body? "I'm sorry," I said. "You've been so loyal, so dependable, so strong and good to me. I'm really sorry. I love you."

How ironic. Here I was, in my mid-sixties, and I appreciated this body more than I did when I was in my twenties and had a stunning, adorable body that I inanely thought was fat and flawed. I saw a Tik-Tok by @Midlifecurious that said, "I am officially pissed off that I spent my skinny years thinking I was fat." Preach, sister! Put it on a T-shirt.

But this morning routine, a mecurial meditation, wasn't just about my body. That was a door I had to pass through. Though I was not immediately aware of the transition taking place, I was beginning to see my private parts, the parts only I could see, and what I saw was a passageway to her, the vulnerable, scared, injured little girl who had been hiding in the way back of me all these years.

Could I reach her? Did I want to?

Now that I had come this far, did I have a choice?

One Sunday, I flew to New York for *The Drew Barrymore Show*. I landed in the afternoon and went straight to CVS to buy some hair color. I wanted to color my roots before the show in the morning. In my hotel room, I walked into the bathroom in my underwear, holding the box of hair color. My reflection stopped me. No makeup. Crappy lighting. Skin that clearly wasn't taut. But I looked . . . strong. Real. Saggy belly, with some muscle underneath. Stretch marks, but soft skin.

Hello, mah sisters.

I liked the way I looked. That in and of itself was a revelation for me. I snapped a selfie and posted it along with a message intended for the pushback I anticipated:

> To all of you that would sit in judgment of my body, the photo, and my reason for posting it, I hope you find a place in your heart to not judge yourself as harshly as you judge others. I have dealt with judgment my entire life starting from when I was a young girl. It has taken me a long time to realize that my judgment, with patient discernment, is the only judgment that counts.
>
> More importantly, what is my character like? Am I kind to people? When I'm not kind, what is in my way? Is it my ego or my emotions? Or both? How can I change and grow to be the best version of me today. In this body.
>
> It's taken me almost three years of emotional labor to get to this point mentally, and for the first eight months of this year I had physical setbacks. I don't care what you think of my body. I don't care what you think about my posting it.

For the first time in my life, I love my body as it is. It's not the twenty-year-old body that I hated and it really is a shame that I hated that beautiful body. Yes, it was a very different body than the one I now inhabit, but it hadn't yet been through the journey I needed to go through. Even as challenging as it's been and is, I am grateful for this journey, and I wouldn't trade this body for my twenty-year-old body any day. Ever.

* * *

The post went viral. Some people applauded. Others gagged. I looked up one man who posted an emoji of a baby throwing up and thought, "Fine, you don't do it for me, either." I'm shocked at the things that don't affect me anymore. Someone wrote, "Oh, you're just doing it because you need your ego stroked." Point taken, and you know what? Maybe I was fishing for a few compliments. Feeling seen isn't a crime.

And if some people were digging it while every lump, bump, wrinkle, and saggy part was exposed, I must have been doing something right.

Drew and her cohost Ross Mathews thought so. With cameras rolling, they immediately brought up my "underwear selfie." They were almost giddy. *Talk about that picture*, they said. Not only did I talk about it, I stood up, lifted my sweater, and gave Drew's audience a closeup of my belly. "You can see all the planks and sit-ups I've done through the years underneath all the saggy skin," I said. "But it's over sixty years of gravity! I'm proud of those little saggies!"

When the audience clapped, I felt they were clapping for more than me. We all live in bodies. We all carry wounds. And we all crave peace. I used to think self-love came from weight loss, from looking a certain way. Now I know it comes from acknowledging those wounds and doing your best to let go or at least learn to live with the shame they cause. The reveal I shared didn't tell the whole story. I didn't know it yet. But I was on my way.

So many of our struggles stem from a condition we all share: the perfectly imperfect nature of being human. We spend more time fighting ourselves than loving ourselves. But there is peace in acceptance. Beauty is found in the calm. Our spirit emerges from the silence.

Getting naked wasn't just physical. It wasn't just about taking off my clothes and staring at my body. It turned out that was the easy part. Which sounds crazy on its face. But it really had nothing to do with the physical. For me, it was spiritual. Emotionally vulnerable. It felt much more exposed. It meant stripping away the stories I'd told myself. It meant letting go of the masks I wore to protect myself. It was about seeing, really seeing, what was underneath, not what I showed others but what only I could see, what I've kept inside—the fears and self-loathing and shame that I've carried around my entire life.

What was left was . . . me.

Raw. Honest.

Naked. And daring myself to look at the truth, the *whole* truth. I had been afraid of knowing myself.

I had come a long way, but the road still stretched ahead. I thought of that line by author Taffy Brodesser-Akner: "You survive what happened to you, then you survive your survival, and then the gift you're given is that you fall in love with your whole life." Yes, that's the goal.

One morning I was looking at myself in the mirror, silently taking inventory, and I glimpsed someone who had eluded me for far too long—that sweet little girl with fear in her eyes. We looked into each other's eyes. She was scared. To her, the world was a field of bees that might sting her. She'd been stung. She asked me if I could help her. I nodded and held out my hand.

"I'll come get you," I said. "We'll walk together. I'll protect you."

sitting still with anger and disappointment (a meditation)

What does it feel like to be peacefully happy?
I feel like I am actively happy,
always putting a good face on in life
because I am so blessed.
So I better damn well be happy!
But what is peaceful happiness like?

JOURNAL ENTRY, JULY 2019

I went into therapy on Saturday thinking about—no, really hung up on—someone who was angry with me. My brain was stuck on this point of fact. I wasn't moving forward, backward, or sideways. I was stuck. My wheels were spinning but taking me nowhere, and I was exhausted from it.

"Please, get me unstuck," I said to my therapist.

"You are holding yourself hostage," she said. "It's not the other person."

"It's me?"

"It's you."

"I'm frustrated and disappointed."

"Why?"

"Someone had a bad experience with me. We both did and I know I can't fix it. I tried. But I'm having trouble moving on."

"Do you hear what you said? It's *you*. You are having trouble moving on."

"What do I do to get unstuck?"

She gave me an exercise:

Sit down and close your eyes.
Breathe deeply and easily. Feel the rhythm of your body, of your heart.
Let the other person walk out of view.
Say goodbye. Say you're sorry it didn't work out as you both had hoped.
When you are alone, take your frustration and your disappointment, take the emotions that you can't let go of, the feelings that are making you feel stuck, and put them in your lap.
Sit in the discomfort of them. Talk to them. Feel them. Ask what they want you to know, to learn, and if no answers come, ask if they are even about you.
Look at them as you breathe.
Are they all of you? No.
Do they define you? No.
Do they mean you are not good and kind? No.
Do they mean you are not lovable? No.
Can you change whatever caused those feelings? No.
Do they prevent you from standing up and walking away into the rest of your life? No.
Breathe deeply and easily.
Feel the rhythm of your body, of your heart.
See yourself as separate from those emotions you've placed in your lap. Pick them up and place them at your feet.

Now stand up, say goodbye to them, tell them you'll talk to them later if they need, and walk away from them . . . into your life.

* * *

Sometimes "the work" we do on ourselves is just sitting in silence and breathing—getting through that discomfort we're feeling and knowing it won't ultimately destroy us, knowing it won't overwhelm us. It's not easy. It's challenging. It's uncomfortable. And it doesn't always work immediately. But the more frequently I do this, the better I feel. Maybe this exercise will help you, too.

smaller and wiser

You can take the safe path
or the brave path.
Be brave.

JOURNAL ENTRY, AUGUST 2023

SOMETHING ABOUT BEING sick when you're alone and you don't want to bother anyone by telling them you are ill, feeling seriously crappy, like maybe borderline 911 crappy, is annoying and pathetic. No one wants to be sick. I hate it. I hate feeling needy. No one wants to deal with thermometers, puss, and bandages—what the nurses call dressing, as if you've turned into a salad. No one wants to call a family member or friend and say, "Hey, I didn't tell you, but I got a boob job—well, a reverse boob job—and it's made me sick."

But that was me. I was lying in bed with a 104-degree fever, infection spreading through my body, and gross stuff dripping out of my right breast. I had gotten my thirty-plus-year-old breast implants removed, and my body was sending me a message. It was upset with me and sounded like the old Chiffon margarine TV commercial: "It's not nice to fool Mother Nature."

It's a lesson I don't mind sharing with the world. Too much of the true, unique beauty of being human gets ignored or distorted through the cultural messaging we receive that there is some ideal of attractiveness that everyone should strive for. It's through all this messaging that we lose sight of the good stuff about ourselves. I'm horrified that I was part of this messaging. I was also one of those women who fell prey to it, seeing only what I imagined was wrong with me.

In my fifties, I experimented with fillers and Botox. I was doing battle against puffy eyes, jowls, saggy skin—basically looking my age. I didn't want to look my age, though I wouldn't have been able to tell you what age I wanted to look. I would've said, "Just younger. Not so tired looking." Don't get me wrong, I am not against plastic surgery or Botox and fillers. Some people look amazing when it works.

They feel much better about themselves after a procedure. I get it—and I've been there.

But no longer. I'm searching for a different kind of beauty, the kind that radiates from the inside out, that comes from living, from being resilient. When I look in the mirror, I want to see all of me staring back—the little girl, the sixteen-year-old on *One Day at a Time*, the twenty-year-old who married too young, the thirty-year-old who gave birth to my son, the fiftysomething who had the time of her life on *Hot in Cleveland*, the cook, the sister, the friend, the mother of the groom, the survivor.

If it takes a bunch of lines and wrinkles to show all that, fine by me. I've never really worn much makeup when not working. Less so as I've gotten older. I am most comfortable in my natural face. In a recent interview, I was asked what my two favorite beauty products are. I said, "Gratitude and wisdom." It sounds corny, but it's truer than ever.

Except I know none of that explains why I was sick in bed after surgery to take out my breast implants. Neither does it explain why I had implants in the first place.

* * *

When it comes to my breasts, I've always had a complicated relationship. A love-hate relationship, you might say—or mostly hate. There's a scene toward the end of one of my favorite movies, *Notting Hill*, with the radiant Julia Roberts in bed with a very charming Hugh Grant—they're finally the lovers they were meant to be—and she asks, "What is it about men and nudity—particularly breasts?"

The question might be better asked by a disciple of Dr. Freud than a gorgeous movie star. Nevertheless, following another attempt at making the shape and function of breasts seem banal, Julia asks again, "What's all the fuss about?" Hugh Grant asks with understated curiosity and charm. "Actually, I can't think what it is really. Let me just have a quick look."

That almost captures the relationship I've had with my breasts. *Let me just have a quick look.* Growing up with three brothers, I always fancied myself a tomboy and therefore hung out in the neighborhood with the boys, roughhousing, fishing, building forts, playing ball in the street. And the stage was set for a complicated relationship between me and my boobs. Mine were mocked relentlessly. They were called "little quarters," "itty-bitty titties," and "tiny boobies." I took it all to heart. Instead of appreciating the changes my body was going through, I dreaded them. I had no idea what I was supposed to look like; I only knew it was wrong.

I was twelve years old when I got my first job, a commercial for JCPenney. I was cast because I fit into the clothes. Which is ironic because I spent the rest of my career dreading fittings because they reminded me of how imperfect I thought I was. At fifteen, I was hired to play the younger daughter on Norman Lear's groundbreaking sitcom *One Day at a Time*. The role, a cute, dorky teenager dealing with the challenges of adolescence, wasn't that much of a stretch from my real life—except that twenty to thirty million people watched me grow up every week.

That might seem like it would have been weird, only it wasn't. Perhaps that was because this all happened pre-Internet, pre-digital, even pre-VCR. I could disappear into my private life when I wasn't working, or, as often happened as we got older, I slipped away with my costar

Mackenzie Phillips for a glass of wine and a cigarette, and no one was the wiser. The weirdness happened years later, when I realized that people who watched the show had a fixed idea of what I looked like. They all grew older, but they wanted to remember me as the teenager they watched on TV after finishing their homework. Over time, and thanks to the Internet, we all reconnected and caught up on our lives. But take it from me, it's a lot more challenging getting older in front of millions of people than it was going through puberty and getting boobs.

In the late '80s, a number of years after I'd married Ed, I was taking an aerobics class and the instructor looked amazing. After class, we were talking, and she mentioned that she'd had a boob job six months earlier. She was clear about it, and proud.* I told her that I might want to have the same procedure if I could look like her. She gave me the name of her doctor. Typical of me, I didn't get a second or third opinion. I met with her plastic surgeon and left after saying, "Let's do it."

I didn't want them to be too big, I told the doctor. "I'm barely a B cup, I'd like to be barely a C. I just want to be fuller." Three weeks later, I was in his operating room, going from between a size A and B to a size D.

* * *

Oh, what I wouldn't give for those cute little boobies back. They were perfect, perky, and beautiful. Why couldn't I see that? Ed was

---

* She was also proud that she existed on seven hundred calories a day. I didn't know how she could do it—I was barely existing on fifteen hundred a day! The pure insanity of not giving our bodies proper nutrition just boggles my mind now. Most of us were brainwashed of any sense when it came to what we need to eat to be healthy and happy.

mystified. "Why?" he asked. He fell in love with me the way I was and couldn't understand when I explained that I got implants because I felt incomplete. He counted two boobs—one, two. What was missing? He sounded like Julia Roberts. "What's all the fuss?"

"This will fix me," I told myself.

I didn't know it then, but I do know now that "fixing" what we look at as external flaws only puts off the inevitable crash. The ghost we see in the mirror pointing out what's wrong with our body is only distracting us from the internal shame I was avoiding working with. I would never feel *fixed* as long as I hesitated looking at what really ailed me. This is the wisdom that comes with age and the frustration of trying to "fix" myself but always feeling like I had failed. It took me a while—decades—to get the message. I think that's true of most women. From early on, we're told by the media, advertising, reality TV, social media, and often people in our lives that we're not complete, not enough, or just short of where we should and could be if only we used the right products or wore the right clothes or spoke to the right doctor. We're trained to look for flaws in ourselves and then to repair, cover up, and rejuvenate.

After I got the implants, I never put them on display. I tried to hide them even, embarrassed that I had done it. Not until I was on *Hot in Cleveland* did they make regular appearances, and that was only because being a little bodacious was part of my character. Of course, by then they were being held up by pulleys and levers after twenty years of weight gain and weight loss. I'm a little envious of those women who can walk a red carpet in next to nothing, knowing their bodies are ripped from the pages of some fantasy of desirability. They're electric. Everybody wants them, men and women. And here, back in reality land, they are probably just as insecure about something none of us notice.

The grass isn't always greener on the other side. In fact, I bet it never is. We all have something keeping us from feeling whole. And it's not our boobs.

*　*　*

By the time *Hot in Cleveland* taped its final episode, age and weight fluctuations had made me look like the *Far Side* cartoon depicting an old woman with breasts drooping like heavy sandbags and nipples next to her belly button. It's an exaggeration, of course; but is it really? Any woman of a certain age understands this. Not only had my boobs lost their perk, they were painful. They were in the way. They didn't fit in my size D bra anymore. Far from it. And my back hurt. Something had to be done.

My breasts were like aging parents whose decline was beyond my ability to care for them any longer. I needed help. This was nothing to be ashamed about; it was real life, albeit inconvenient, but hey, it wasn't that different from having to change the batteries in your smoke detectors at 2 a.m. It was just more complicated—and expensive. Instead of running out to CVS to get batteries, I would need surgery.

To quote the great journalist Linda Ellerbee, "And so it goes." Life happens when you're solving problems. Everything else is a hot fudge sundae.

I meant to consult a doctor about doing the procedure, but I put it off while enjoying a relatively carefree window in my life, my hot fudge sundae, as it were. Then one day I was screwing around at my son's house—the same house where I had lived with Ed when Wolfie was born. Wolfie had to do a radio interview but was sound asleep in his bed.

His wife and I tiptoed in the bedroom to wake him. I stole his phone, and he chased after me. I sprinted down the stairs, tripped, and landed on my right boob. I heard a pop. I knew exactly what had happened.

The irony was that I had feared falling on those stairs ever since I was pregnant with Wolfie. I'd had them built a million years ago, and they had given me nightmares ever since. Now that fear became a reality. I had a consultation with a plastic surgeon who I found through a friend. I said something to the effect of, "I want my little boobies back."

He did his exam and explained the procedure. He cautioned me about potential difficulty in cleaning out the ruptured implant. He also made sure I understood that I would still need new implants even though the old ones were being removed. "Small, though," I said. "As long as you don't make 'em big again, let's do it."

Six weeks later, I had the surgery. My doctor showed me the old implants. They were like ostrich eggs, hard and crusted over. Lovely imagery, I know. I couldn't believe they had been in my body. I went home bandaged and sore, with drains under my arms, uncomfortable but hopeful. For the first two weeks, everything was great. I went for hyperbaric oxygen therapy every other day to help heal faster. I laid in the plexiglass tank and watched *Outlander* on the TV screen above the chamber.

And hello?! Would it have hurt somebody to have warned me about the last two episodes of the first season. Good Christ. They are absolutely diabolical and terrifying.

My next checkup seemed routine. The bandages came off, the tubes came out, and I stood in front of the mirror, grinning from ear to ear. "I have my old boobies back," I said, beaming. They weren't in the way. I could move my arms. I could actually see the skin under my breasts without holding them up. Now nothing was blocking my view. Who knew I had a birthmark there under my right breast?

"This is fabulous!" I said.

About a week later my right breast took on shades of green, yellow, and blue. The next day it started to swell and turned a dark purple. I felt myself getting dizzy. By nighttime, I was running a fever.

I stayed in bed, figuring that was best, Tylenol and lots of water and tea. Whenever I got up, though, the pain was intense, my breast was throbbing, and it kept getting worse. I knew I had to see the doctor, but it was Saturday morning. I decided to wait until Monday. By then, I was really sick. My breast was discolored, painful, and swollen. I was burning up. I had fluid leaking out of the sutures around my nipple.

The doctor saw me that morning. I could tell by the look on his face that I was in trouble. I heard him call the other doctor who saw me for aftercare and whisper in the hall about putting me on antibiotics. He arranged for me to immediately go to the aftercare clinic for intravenous antibiotics and have that doctor take a look. "I'm sending her now," I overheard him say. "Yes, this is an emergency." The next place was close by. There, the doctor examined my infected breast and said, "Yeah, this implant has to come out right away." I was in surgery the next morning. Three and a half weeks after my first surgery.

* * *

I called Wolfie right away to see if he could drive me the next morning and made it sound like it was just a hiccup, nothing to worry about. I remember being bummed about missing a tribute concert to Bon Jovi the day after that second surgery. Wolfie was performing in it. But saner heads, namely my son and his wife and my brother Patrick, persuaded me to stay home and rest. The have-you-lost-your-mind looks they gave me all said the same thing: "What part about almost dying from an infection don't you get?"

The second surgery involved removing the implant and the infection from the tissue surrounding the muscle. Recovery took more time. Then my boob started to fall in on itself. The doctor referred to it as cratering. The description was accurate. Another apt word was *gross*. Like, really gross. It looked like a horror movie—and it was. I had an open wound the size of a misshaped quarter and a hole more than an inch deep where my nipple used to be. My nipple, or what was left of it, was holding on to within a literal half inch of its life. I went into the doctor's office every day so they could clean the wound, flush it out, snip out the dying tissue, and repack it with antibiotic ointments, gauze, and bandages and who knows what else.

My poor right breast needed, at minimum, six months to heal the infection, close the wound, and grow back some of the missing tissue. A third surgery seven months after the first one installed another small implant under the muscle and restored what was left of my nipple. By the end of the year, my boobs were, uh, slowly taking shape. Sort of. They are now two completely different sizes, the implant on the left is over the muscle, and my right side is sad and misshapen. (But it's the small size I always wanted! Cloud, lining . . .) Eventually I will have a fourth operation that will, I am assured, even things out once and for all.

I didn't want to think about when that would happen, and I still don't. Four surgeries in one year was quite enough for me, thank you very much.* But something to look forward to? Eventually, I'll be on Medicare and my perky new boobs will be ready for the high school prom.

---

* Ten days before my third breast surgery, I had surgery to remove a fractured molar. Fun times.

In all seriousness, I'm lucky to have survived. That weekend scared the piss out of me. After a lifetime of always thinking I needed to fix something about myself, this last go-round has been a doozie. It's been a test. Through it all, I've seen my breasts in states that I'd never imagined—and all in an effort to get them back to the way they were before I thought bigger would be better. Jane Austen was right when she wrote in *Emma*, "Vanity working on a weak head produces every sort of mischief."

It hasn't been easy physically or psychologically, but I've slowly found my way to forgiveness, acceptance, and equanimity by finding the beauty inside me. I learned a lesson the way we learn almost everything, the hard way, by making a mistake, and I have the scars as proof. And my son, his wife, my family, my girlfriends—what a blessing to have them in my life. They never made me feel needy. They were all there for me. They never touched that unspoken childhood wound. They just loved me. Simply. Without judgment. When I needed it the most.

One morning, I walked outside in my backyard. Bandaged but on the rebound, I took baby steps through my garden. I looked at the flowers and the trees, standing tall and short, reaching up and branching out, all gorgeous, but none alike. Every single one was unique in its beauty. No one shape, color, or pattern exactly alike.

That's the way Mother Nature works. When we aren't blind to her genius, if we aren't questioning her or trying to fool her, her answers to our questions are right in front of us.

never say never

Even now, at my age, my heart remains tender, timid, hopeful, and hungry. It is also the most resilient part of me.

JOURNAL ENTRY, JANUARY 2025

We are born in relationship,
we are wounded in relationship,
and we can be healed in relationship.
—HARVILLE HENDRIX, *GETTING THE LOVE YOU WANT*

I HAVE GONE on record—more than once—saying that I'm done with love. At this stage of the game, I figured the rest of my life would be content, calm, and solo: my cats and Luna curled on the couch, my crossword puzzles and novels stacked on the side table, and leftovers for dinner at four thirty. If I'm lucky, grandchildren will occupy me. I have let certain people know I'm on call for hugs and babysitting.

But romantic love? Oof. Over it. Been there, done that. Screw the stigma of always being a singleton.

"Will there be a plus-one?"

"Not in this lifetime, thanks."

My second divorce closed that chapter for good. I held it together more or less during that heartbreak. I finished my cooking show with a smile, I went to food festivals, and I didn't fall apart when the sitcom pilot I shot didn't get picked up. I even managed to keep all my plants alive and never once drove off with the gas nozzle still in my tank. I mean, that's worth something, right?

But truth be told, emotionally, I was like a shaky Jenga tower—one tug away from collapse. How had I ended up divorced twice? There are thousands of books, podcasts, and videos about grief and loss, but few address what it feels like to be a two-time loser in love. I grew up watching *The Mary Tyler Moore Show*. Mary Richards was the ultimate career woman of the '70s. She worked hard. She could turn the world on with her smile. She never married. Maybe that was the key.

Except real-life Mary was married three times. Once more than me. Maybe the secret is you keep saying "I do" until it sticks.

Like Betty White, who also married three times. The first two were brief (she called them "rehearsals"), while the third, to her beloved Allen Ludden, ended when he died after eighteen years of wedded bliss. He was only fifty-nine years old when he passed; she never remarried. "When you've had the best, who needs the rest?" she explained. She kept a photo of Allen on her nightstand and blew him a kiss every morning. At night, she sent a kiss toward the heavens. She had no doubt they would reunite in the afterlife. The last word she said before she died was "Allen."

My own mother got married at seventeen and stayed married through thick and thin. She made a promise and kept it. Maybe that was the key.

Me? I got to a point where I threw my hands up. "Basta." I couldn't crack the code of lasting love. Romance has never been easy for me, never even sane. It's a messy math equation—love, marriage, divorce—and I'm terrible at math. Worse at marriage. Ed and I were amicable through the most difficult times of our split. We hurt each other's feelings, but we always tried to do the right thing.

Finding myself divorced a second time hit so hard. The flood of questions afterward blindsided me. I thought what I had with Tom was love, but after we split, I found myself debating whether the love had been real. I doubted myself. I dove into full-on, full-time healing: Rolfing, Pilates, long walks, therapy, cryotherapy, gaining weight, releasing weight, ugly-crying in the basement, forgiving people who hurt me, forgiving myself for bad decisions, giving up alcohol, trying acupuncture, lymphatic drainage, infrared saunas, energy work, endless Rumi quotes on Instagram, kitten and baby goat videos on TikTok. I did it all.

The silver lining? Growth, strength, maybe even wisdom. But I was waking up and going to bed alone, shopping for one, and changing my own light bulbs. I knew it was probably best to keep it that way to prevent another slip on the banana peel of amore. It was safe, and I was down for safe.

Then something happened that changed my mind . . .

* * *

In April 2023, I flew to Amsterdam to see my son and his band, Mammoth, open for Metallica, the kickoff of their huge M72 World Tour. Sixty thousand people packed the Johan Cruijff Arena. The pride I felt for my hardworking, talented kid was written all over my face—I couldn't stop smiling during his eleven-song set, which included songs from Mammoth's just-released second album.

It was a special mom moment: I mean, if I closed my eyes, I could still easily picture him playing goalie on his AYSO soccer team on Saturday mornings, with me and Ed and the parents of his teammates cheering on the sidelines each time he blocked a shot. Now tens of thousands of people were singing along to his songs, recording him on their phones, and clapping for an encore. I screamed for more with them. Even better? His wife, whom I adore, was beaming with pride right next to me.

How did I get so lucky? My son was in a loving relationship and thriving creatively. He was happy. It was everything I'd hoped for when he was growing up. The only part missing? His dad. But Ed knew Wolf's success was inevitable before he passed. He'd been his biggest cheerleader (next to me) and watched him take off on his own. And I believe, in some way, he was present.

After the encore, I went backstage and hugged Wolf for both of us, then waited for Metallica to go on. Now, I've seen way too many rock concerts, so it takes a lot to get me excited, but I actually had goose bumps before Metallica went on—but not for a reason anyone would have guessed.

Earlier that day, I had been hanging out in Wolf's trailer backstage. The door was open, letting afternoon sunlight stream in. The mood was chill. Suddenly, this tall, beautiful man stepped in front of the door, blocking the light. It was Metallica's lead singer and songwriter, James Hetfield. He had stopped by to say hi to Wolf and the band. He saw me sitting on a chair in the corner and got a big grin on his face as Wolfie started to introduce us.

"You're Valerie Bertinelli!" he said. "I know you!"

My heart skipped a beat. I knew who he was, too. I'd seen photos. But I had no idea he was this handsome. In person, he was even taller, more rugged. I forgot about him while Mammoth was onstage. Then, around 9 p.m., normally the time I'm winding down with a book and my pillow, I went out to the floor with Wolfie and his bandmates to watch Metallica. From the opening song, the pounding instrumental "Orion," the music took hold of me and never let go.

So did their man out front. I had never seen Metallica live, but I could tell that I wasn't the only woman in the arena feeling this way. Watching James play his electric V-shaped guitar was sparking a fancy I was nowhere near even considering. In a black shirt and jeans, he exuded strength, power, and charisma as he leaned into the microphone and sang "For Whom the Bell Tolls." I pumped my right arm in the air along with everyone else. I couldn't contain myself—and didn't want to.

No man had crossed my mind in this way in what felt like forever. I just assumed the limerence train was never traveling through these parts again. But now my mind was like a steamy romance novel I was writing in real time. How about that, Mama Wolf's pilot light was still lit. Who'da thunk it?

Hours later, I saw James again backstage at a dinner the band has after every show. The perfect host, he welcomed us to their feast. The magnetism that had captivated tens of thousands for the past three hours was still evident, a force that took some time getting used to that close up, and yet he was open and accessible, interested and inviting conversation. We talked about sobriety and divorce. We laughed. I also met his lovely girlfriend, who was beautiful, kind, and charming on her own.

At the airport the next day, I told my brother Patrick about my mini crush on James and how nice it was to know I'm not completely dead inside. He teased me, as brothers do, and didn't stop for months. By then, I was no longer thinking about James, but I was thinking about romance. Was there really a man out there who could make me feel that way? If there was, would we find each other? Would he be single? Straight? Would the timing be right? How would I know it was him? Was I going to have to date? Would anyone want to date me?

OMG! Where was my eighth grade yearbook when I needed it? Suddenly, I was fourteen years old again. Help!

* * *

It dawned on me that I have never been on a first date. I am in my mid-sixties and no one has ever called and asked me out, told me what time they'd pick me up, and arranged to have dinner or go for a walk on the beach, or whatever else people do on first dates. I met my second husband at a charity dinner in Scottsdale. We texted and got together whenever I visited my parents in Arizona.

I met Ed backstage at a concert and hung out at his hotel until he left town. He called me three days later, invited me to visit him on the road, and we were together from then on.

And the guy who took my virginity in high school? We never dated. We went to football games and made out in his pickup truck.

I recently found a diary I kept in 1975, when I was fifteen years old. Rehearsals for *One Day at a Time* had started, but the show hadn't aired yet, so I was still in public school and anonymous. My diary was like a best friend. "Wait, I have to get into my pajamas," I wrote one night. "OK, I'm back. Where was I?"

I was talking about boys.

What else are diaries for at that age?

Most of my entries were about one of two boys. There was Peter, apparently a good friend with whom I spent hours talking on the phone at night, though sadly I don't remember him. Then there was Jeff, who I pined after. I remember him. He was with a girl named Meg but leading me on. "Today was the dance after school," I wrote. "Jeff danced with me once because he felt sorry for me. He thought I was crying over him. That's a laugh! I wasn't!"

A few weeks later: "I haven't heard from Jeff since last Monday," I wrote. "Doesn't matter that much. There're lots of cute guys at Granada."

A year later my first serious boyfriend dropped me. I thought my life was over at sixteen years old. A few weeks later I was looking out for cute boys on the studio lot where *One Day at a Time* was shot. What happened to that resiliency? Age, I suppose. The end of my marriage to Ed after twenty-plus years was painfully hard, though our commitment to Wolfie and each other remained and love returned in a different, not intimate, but maybe an even deeper way than before. I'm grateful for that and still trying to figure it out.

The end of my second marriage left me angry—angry at him, angry at the legal system, and angrier at myself.

But I did love the man at one point. Where did that love go? What happens to love when it's gone? How could I have continued to feel love for Ed after our divorce but have no feelings—neither good nor bad—for my second husband after fifteen years of togetherness? Hopefully that will change over time. I can already feel myself softening. I've reached a point of indifference and grace, which is so much healthier than hanging on to anger.

The truth is, nothing stays the same, including love. Our heart is like the universe. It doesn't have walls. It can hold different types of love for many people. I love my son. I love my daughter-in-law. I loved and still love Ed. I love my brothers. I love my father, though understanding that love has been a challenge. My mother's the same. I've learned to let myself feel the feelings and be open to the paradoxes.

Love is a feeling, and feelings change over time. They evolve. We evolve. Feelings are all energy, and energy doesn't stagnate. It moves.

* * *

From the time I left that Metallica concert, though, I felt something was missing from my life. I was craving *something* the way I did when Ed was on the road early in our marriage and I missed the way he would wrap himself around me in bed. Or was I craving something the way I craved Italian sub sandwiches when I was pregnant?

No, I was hungry but not for food. I hadn't felt like this for so long I'd forgotten exactly what it was that I desired. And when I did remember, I said exactly two words to myself: "Oh shit."

I wanted a hug. I just wanted a real hug. I wanted the comfort of a hug from someone . . .

I wanted to feel loved by someone other than my son, my family, and my girlfriends. I wanted to feel seen and appreciated, wanted, and loved for the complex, contradictory, imperfect, vulnerable, mushy soul that I am. And I wanted to return that love. With my whole heart. I wanted someone to feel safe in *my* arms. I have a lot of love in me to share. A line I once read came back to me: "One can live alone, but one cannot be human alone." There was no shortage of hugs in my life—from family and friends. But it's different when that hug comes from someone lying next to you at night.

In her memoir *Committed: A Skeptic Makes Peace with Marriage*, Elizabeth Gilbert wrote, "To be fully seen by somebody, then, and be loved anyhow—this is a human offer that can border on the miraculous." Yes, a thousand times yes! I told myself that I deserved the miraculous, and of course, I was right.

We all deserve it.

But why do I resist love when, like breath and sleep, it is so clearly essential to the full and healthy experience of being human?

Fear of the crushing pain we suffer when love goes away is one reason. A broken heart is a pain unlike any other, especially when you include the pain of attorney fees and settlement payouts after a divorce. Breakups are the number one cause of lopsided haircuts, long phone conversations with girlfriends, binge eating, and countless hours of scrolling through Netflix for a movie that will inspire a belief in love again.*

The other reason? Me. The failure of past relationships has made me comfortably gun-shy. It's easier and safer to say no and avoid past mistakes than it is to say yes and enter the unknown. I also like being alone. I have a big, busy, bonkers career. I'm pretty set in my ways, too. I sleep with cats. I wake up and scroll through my phone before I get out of bed. I need a cup of coffee in the morning before I communicate with anyone. I'm a lot. Too much? I don't think so.

I suppose that's for someone else to decide.

* * *

But I was softening. Was I ready to look for a new friend? A partner? Or did I just want a summerlong duet with a Danny Zuko of my own?

The Olivia Newton-John–John Travolta thing wasn't going to work for me. I didn't have flings in my younger days; there was no reason to change now that I qualified as a senior at the movie theater. What about my long-standing Cinderella fantasy? Prince Charming

---

* Try these: *Everafter, Notting Hill, Moonstruck, Groundhog Day, You've Got Mail, While You Were Sleeping* . . .

would show up on my doorstep with a glass flip-flop I'd left at the beach. Unfortunately, I hadn't been to the beach for a long time. A dating app? No frickin' way—though I did have some fun imagining my profile:

> Must love animals, be kind, witty, emotionally intelligent, gentle but burly, preferably tall and dark, with maybe a graying beard, but that's not a dealbreaker. And I'll be the same for you. (Okay, I'm not tall, but my mustache is graying. Does that count?) Allergic to cats? Sorry, you're out. You should also understand Sundays are sacred—spent communing with Wordle, Connections, the crossword, and the NFL.

"How about the *Golden Bachelorette?*" a friend asked, jokingly (I think). "It would be you and twenty-four guys."

The thought made me shudder. I have no problem kissing five cats throughout the day and a few at night, but even half that number of guys—and on television—gives me the heebie-jeebies. Besides, it wouldn't be exciting or titillating TV. I'd spend half the show looking for my ChapStick and the other half for my glasses so I could see who I was supposed to date. I really don't think people should compete for love. I believe a connection is there or it's not, and if it is, the odds of that turning into love, the kind of easy, long-lasting love most of us want, is not just small but minuscule. No one should have to sell themselves as hard as people do on those dating shows.

I could possibly meet someone while waiting for samples of artichoke and jalapeño dip at Costco. Why not? Have you seen the crowds around those sample tables? It's like a bar, only a little rowdier, and you don't have to be embarrassed if you show up at 10 a.m. Or a friend or one of my brothers might try to set me up. They'll sense a guy is right and let him know what's what. "Val's great. If you can make her laugh, you're in. If you hurt her, we'll kill you."

I'm not joking. As a lot of women in my situation will attest, it's hard to find love at this age. Further, at this age, we have to ask, what is love?

* * *

Then it happened. In the spring of 2024, I was in Trader Joe's of all places, minding my own business as I pushed my cart up and down the aisles. I stopped in the produce section to respond to a text, then resumed my shopping in the pantry aisle, the one with dried fruit and chocolate and other treats. And there I fell in love.

They say love happens on its own, when you least expect it, when you aren't looking for it, and in my case, all the above was true. It wasn't a meet-cute, like in the movies. I went home first; that's where I opened the pack of Trader Joe's Trio of Soft Licorice Twists Raspberry, Mango, and Green Apple. I picked up a bag on a lark and I knew instantly. The taste was sublime, pure, natural. It was love at first bite. Like classic Van Halen. "And then you sense a change, nothin' feels the same . . . love comes walkin' in."

As for finding Mr. Right, I had better luck picking tomatoes at my local farmers' market. The object of dating is simple. It was drummed into my head as a little girl when I played the Milton Bradley board game Mystery Date. You collected cards with pieces of different-colored outfits on them. After getting a matching outfit, you were ready for your date. A door in the center of the board hid five guys. Four were cool. You wanted to avoid the fifth, the dud! And forgive me, but I never saw anything wrong with the dud. He was cute!

My divorces notwithstanding, that taught me everything I needed to know. Up to a point. It's more complicated later in life. You need more than good looks, cute outfits, and handsome smiles. Provided you get over the hurdle of meeting someone who might—and I emphasize that word, *might*—inspire you to clean out a drawer and free up a few hangers in your closet, you then have to spend time with them. Dinner, a walk, responding to their texts in a reasonable amount of time . . . see, it's already complicated.

Anyway, once you get past whether to have dinner at a French bistro or your favorite neighborhood Thai place, you then must make conversation with each other—and at this age, you both bring baggage to the table. Exes, kids, stepkids, former jobs, illnesses, body parts that don't work anymore, past surgeries, upcoming surgeries, questions about whether you can eat grapefruit with the medication you're taking, and so on. Talking about favorite TV shows and movies is out, because who can remember the titles or the names of actors anymore? Bone density issues? Hormone replacement therapy? Best to save those topics for . . . later.

I have met less than a handful of men over the past two years who have at least made me wonder if I had room for someone else's ego, never mind their breakfast cereal and bath towels. If conversation with them went well, I would ask myself whether this could turn into something. Was I more interested in a long-term relationship or long-term care? Or were they the same? Was I looking for love or companionship? Was it possible to have love without companionship?

These questions answer themselves over time. I knew they would for me if I got enough chances. I do want that cuddle at night and hug in the morning. I hope someday to find it. In fact, get in touch if you know someone who seems right. I'm kidding. Please don't.

* * *

I had a dream about Ed. The two of us were in a house I didn't recognize—one that felt like a new chapter for both of us. I wanted him to feel loved by me and for that love to seep into his being. It was strange. I was overcome with a deep sense of peace, compassion, and big, aching love for him—and I wanted to share it. I wanted to help him deal with his grief and trauma the way I have been getting through mine. I wanted to ensure he wasn't in pain.

I believe he knew how I felt when he was alive, and I told him directly toward the end. Ours was a flawed love, but it was real. I knew him for forty years. Even when we were angry, we stayed loving. It changed, evolved, and grew back different but stronger than it had been at the beginning of our relationship. It healed us.

But my dream wasn't just about Ed—it was also about me. About remembering that love doesn't end. It evolves. That when I say never, what I really mean is not yet. Because the truth is, I still believe in the miraculous. I still want the miraculous.

No matter how long or short it lasts, intimate love feels like nothing else in the world. The pain of heartbreak doesn't come anywhere close to the bliss. Love is magical. Love is intoxicating. Love is calm.

Love is intense. Love is quiet. Love is dangerous. Love is safe. Love is playful. Love is letting someone see you, all of you, naked and afraid, naked and silly, naked and giving, naked and sexy, just naked, and being told that is beautiful.

And if there's one thing I've learned?

Never say never.

connections

Our life is a tempest of moments and memories. Wear them like a beautiful necklace.

JOURNAL ENTRY, APRIL 2024

SOMETIMES YOU NEED a hug. Most of life's problems have only one tried-and-true solution, and that's the passage of time. What's the phrase? Time heals all wounds. I couldn't resist looking it up. The saying is attributed to a Greek playwright in 300 BCE, though it may have been around a lot longer than that. I suspect that's true. Probably some mama back when people still lived in caves had a kid who came home one day in tears after being dropped by a friend and said, "It hurts now but over time it will get better. Time heals all wounds."

I have a friend whose grandparents lived in Europe during World War II. They remember bombs being dropped on homes and apartment buildings where they lived. One struck their neighbor's home. They heard a ground-shaking explosion. Everyone inside was killed. My friend's grandparents were huddled together with their family in a corner, terrified, crying, praying, and waiting for time to pass. I can't imagine, and yet I can. We see such scenes on the news almost every day. I am regularly in tears as I sit in front of the screen. Like all of us, I get so angry. "God, why is this happening?"

I say that more from a place of exasperation than a direct conversation with God, but then I think to myself, "Oh, God wants us to see this horrific killing, the fear, and the suffering. We can't be blind to it. We are supposed to acknowledge this part of human nature, this part of our own nature, the dark that contrasts and competes with the light we seek. We are supposed to feel a connection with people we don't know whether they are blocks away or on the other side of the world. We are supposed to feel them in our heart. We are supposed to cry for them as if they are our own neighbors. We are supposed to see ourselves and recognize how similar we are, before we are going through the same thing. We are supposed to do better, find solutions, and stop the killing."

CONNECTIONS

We have never been more connected or able to connect with family and friends and even strangers than we are today. We are a click and a comment away from hundreds of millions of people. Yet many people feel more disconnected, isolated, and depressed than ever before. Has technology done this? When I was growing up, I had two ways of connecting with friends: the rotary phone in our kitchen—the one with the long cord that let you walk around, except that it was always twisted—and my bicycle. It worked. I was never bored and knew what everyone was up to.

Today I was parked in front of the grocery store, in tears, feeling like I was going out of my head. I had an upsetting phone call on the way to stock up after being out of town for work. Then came a barrage of text messages. I couldn't handle it. I had a long grocery list in my purse; it did not include a mental breakdown. I needed better boundaries in my life, I thought. I also needed . . . well, I wanted to numb the way I felt, which meant buying some gin and olives, a few bags of chips, maybe some fried chicken, and half of the cheese section.

But the rational side of my brain intervened and told the emotional side, "No, no, no, we don't do that anymore." Instead I walked out of the grocery store carrying a nine-pound seedless watermelon. Few things can top the sugary taste of a perfectly ripe watermelon, and the one I bought was perfect. I perched my phone against a vase on the kitchen counter and recorded myself cutting it up. I wanted to share the goodness of fresh summer fruit on Instagram and TikTok. I ended up sharing the tough time I was going through, too.

Watermelon and tears. They aren't on anyone's summer menu. But that's what I served to strangers on social media. Why not call a friend? I did. From the parking lot. And she listened to me cry and sniffle my way through this episode until she was convinced that I was headed for the produce section, not the liquor and junk food aisle.

Why also post on social media? For me, it's a way to connect with people who for one reason or another are interested in my life. I've been on TV forever, like fiftysomething years. Many people say they've grown up with me. What they don't realize is the same is true of me. I've grown up with them. The connection is real. Social media has given us the opportunity to connect.

For me, posting has become a way to say, *Here's what's real in my life right now*, and to connect with a community that sees me. I also see them. I respond to many, some online, some privately. It's not just scrolling and liking and double-tapping. It's pen pals, confidants, a chorus of familiar hearts chiming in from across the world. We may not know each other's middle names or coffee orders, but we *know* each other in the ways that count.

We're there for each other. We give each other the confidence to fight the battles within ourselves.

"Feel your feelings," I wrote between bites of watermelon. "Do your best not to numb them. Feelings are information. Ask what they need."

"Don't give in to your cravings!" One woman said this had been a tough month for her, too, one with lots of tears. Another woman said she had recently been diagnosed with Alzheimer's and had been happy from the minute she heard her diagnosis: "Happy like all the time! Why? I have no idea. But I wish this feeling for everyone." I mean, WOW. What a phenomenal woman. Another wrote that her fiancé had just died but left his cat to her, and seeing the cat put a smile on her face. "He knows I have her and am going to love her as much as he did."

I need no more proof that we are in this thing called life together, and we crave the togetherness. Sometimes all we want is to be seen.

Other times being heard is enough. Get the bad stuff off your chest. Then eat watermelon.

* * *

Social media is a great gateway to vulnerability. There's something safe about opening up to people from a distance. I can be vulnerable knowing I can turn it off or block someone who's rude. Curation of friends and followers is imperfect, sometimes potentially dangerous, but over time connections do form, and the caring and advice and sharing that goes on is real. You find that you're not the only one freaking out about something or feeling helpless, alone, or so happy you need to scream. You find kindred spirits, people who went through the same thing or feel the same way. You share thoughts, info, and insights. You offer each other support. I remember when Ed was going through his cancer treatments, a woman messaged me on Facebook. She was going through the same thing, and we traded information. These connections are like Band-Aids. A smiley face emoji can be a light in the darkness. *I see you. You see me.* We aren't as alone as we might think, and that in itself can be helpful or healing, enough to get us through a hard moment.

Very often what you learn—what I've learned—is that I feel much better when I'm heard and understood. There are people who have your back and you have theirs. These are real friends—and as much as I post on social media, nothing can beat getting together in person. Friendship is the medicine that goes straight to the heart. Even though I profess to be a happy hermit, I need a regular dose of it.

I have been known to ignore this when I have deep wounds to lick, and I feel most comfortable doing it in private. I don't want people to hear my voice and think, "Oh, another woe-is-me story is coming.

What is it this time?" The truth is, more often than not, misery doesn't want company—even though it's best when it has it. And I was taught at a young age to not be needy. I do take some pride in handling things on my own. Being independent, resilient.

But I was worn down and embarrassed. I didn't want my girlfriends to see what I was going through. Mind you, these were women I'd met when Wolfie was in elementary school. They knew me often better than I knew myself, and for good reason. For almost three decades, we have been resources for each other through braces and bar mitzvahs, divorce, medical scares, deaths, weddings, grandchildren, menopause, and Medicare. Our bonds are solid, understanding, and unbreakable.

I still accepted dinner invites. Celebrated birthdays. Participated on our group text. I was there but not there. As one of them later said to me, I was hiding in plain sight. I'm good at that. It was like dieting. I was starving myself of friendship, advice, support, and unconditional love—and at a time when that was exactly what I needed. I'm going to say there's never a time when we don't need that.

I think this is why I took to social media. I could be vulnerable without looking at it in the face. Or having someone look back at my face. I didn't have that vulnerability mirrored back at me. I could block people. I could choose to ignore the comments. I could get something off my chest without feedback if I so desired, and feel better.

But it wasn't the same. Just as taking an online quiz about mental health isn't the same as talking to my therapist. I was missing a human touch. Like the Springsteen song: "I just want someone to talk to / And a little of that human touch."

My friend Jo knew a bit of what was going on because I dropped Luna off at her house when I traveled. I talked, and she listened without judgment. We hugged. I wanted more. I reconnected with my other girlfriends in that same way. At a dinner get-together, someone brought up two books we had read in book club, both of which I had loved: Geraldine Brooks's excellent novel *Horse* and her memoir of grief following her husband's sudden death, *Memorial Days*. Something about our discussion opened me up. I started talking about what I'd been going through.

It was so weird I refrained from letting this group in on my struggles for such a long time. Now I couldn't stop sharing with them. I apologized to them. I didn't want them to see what I was going through. Of course, they might not have known all the details, but I wasn't fooling them. They knew. They listened. We all cried. They closed ranks around me. We hugged—and yes, I needed those hugs.

I let myself be enveloped by their friendship. I melted inside their arms. I sat amid the safety of our connection. It felt stronger and more intimate than ever before.

"I love you guys," I said, after drying my eyes one more time.

I wasn't the only one holding wads of tissues.

That evening didn't change me as much as it reminded me of something important. My friends are amazing people. If they loved me, there must be something about me that really was worth loving. They got me back on track. Since then, I send them notes, DM them, or leave messages. "Hey, just a gentle reminder that I love you ladies, and I'm so grateful that you are in my life."

Friendship makes you feel that way.

* * *

"I didn't know how I was going to get through it, but knew that *somehow*, I would."

The words weren't mine. But they might as well have been. I came across that sentence on someone's Instagram page. It was two days before Thanksgiving, and that line captured the way I had felt for months. Definitely something to be grateful for. It also marked a personal milestone for me, something that had once seemed beyond reach. But I made it, and I posted about it.

> Today marks two years of freedom. Two years of walking through self-doubt and doing my best to get to the other side. Two years of working through shame and self-loathing. (I'm still working on it.) Two years of working to find my true self. Two years of confronting past demons and traumas and doing my best to work through them.*
>
> I want to be the best, most authentic version of myself heading into this last chapter of my life.

It's always a risk to share so honestly and openly. When I first started on social media—Facebook, then Instagram, and then TikTok—I was guarded. I put up only recipes and photos of my cats. Occasionally something personal slipped through, and those were the posts that received the most authentic feedback. That motivated me to share more personal stories. I still showed up smiling with my cats, but when I didn't feel like smiling, I said so. People related.

This latest post followed suit. Thousands of people responded, but one comment stood out. It said, "You're perfect the way you are, Ma!"

---

* Update: I'm still working on everything I wrote in that post. It's the long-tail effort to know and be okay with me, all of me. The work doesn't stop. It doesn't get easier. It doesn't require fewer tissues. But it does get more interesting. More fulfilling. Don't run from the hard stuff. Lean in. Understand. Don't hide or disparage. Look for insight, clarity, and light. In the light, you will see your truth—and the truth is your lightsaber.

* * *

I hadn't yet finished eating watermelon when a friend of mine called. She's a remarkable woman. Her early life was one challenge after another, all before the age of eight. She survived, then thrived. Her work has taken her around the world, and she's seen it all and then some and has blossomed into one of the kindest souls I've ever known. She's been through hell, and all she wants to do is give back, to be of service. She finds it therapeutic, restorative, uplifting, depending on her mood.

A while ago she got me involved in volunteering at a food bank close to home, and I went there after we finished chatting and I put away the watermelon. Given the tears I'd spilled in the grocery store parking lot and the tumult I'd felt the past few days, I needed to volunteer. I had been too focused on myself. I needed to step outside of and beyond my navel-gazing. I needed to be busy. How does that old *Captain Kangaroo* song go? "Busy hands are happy hands, hands that can't go wrong."

I needed to connect with other people even though I wouldn't ever know who was on the receiving end of the packages I helped fill. I needed connection. And I needed to feel purposeful, like I was being of service. I was given the job of separating food into items that needed to be cooked and those that didn't and bagging the non-cooked food. I was surrounded by boxes and people. It felt good—and so did I.

Somehow, I hoped the people on the receiving end of these packages would know they were seen. I tried to imagine them opening the boxes and feeling less alone. I was among several dozen people just in this room who cared.

We were in this together. We are all in this thing called life together. We might never meet, but it is important to know we are connected.

and yet

Let's try another way.
Instead of fear, try love.
Instead of pain, try compassion.
Instead of darkness, try light.

JOURNAL ENTRY, MARCH 2025

Every secret has a unique weight to it,
and you can only carry them for so long.
—DEREK DELGAUDIO, *IN & OF ITSELF*

OUR MINDS CONTAIN many different rooms—places where we store experiences, hang our thoughts, and shelter our emotions. There are rooms we enter when we're happy, scared, lonely, and exhausted. Rooms we slip into when we want to go to sleep. Some rooms are quiet and peaceful. Some are chaotic and loud. Others are off-limits. Like many people, I have as many rooms as I do different and conflicted voices in my head.

I didn't begin to explore this idea until I went through a stretch when I was unable to quiet my mind and felt anxious and out of control. In therapy, I learned to build a new room in my head where I could feel safe, protected from things that made me feel exposed and vulnerable.

I pictured a beautiful room with a very heavy door that only I could open. Inside, a cloud of pillows was piled on a warm corduroy sofa brownish-burgundy in color. Across the room, a fire crackled in the fireplace. Through a large window, a soft snow was falling outside. Beyond the snow were trees and mountaintops. It was both heaven and haven.

It took a lot of work in therapy to finally get to and construct that room, and then to open the door. Nearly ten years. The first time I stepped inside, I discovered a little girl already there, alone, reading her favorite book. She was me. And, for decades, she had helped the adult me survive. Now it was my turn to help her.

She looked up at me, wide-eyed and hopeful.

"It's going to be okay," I told her.

I'm still trying to convince her it's true.

* * *

Therapy has helped enormously, but making myself feel safe—and helping that little girl feel safe—requires trust and belief, something that hinged on me. I never realized I held that power. I assumed the physical work I was doing—like when I hit that magic number on the scale, met *the* guy, or went *x* number of months without a drink—would do the healing for me, and one day, I'd wake up feeling . . . healed.

But each time I returned to that room, I knew the truth. I couldn't keep my promise to her without facing the wound that started it all:

When I was eleven years old, I was sexually abused.

I feel the pain just writing that sentence. That little girl and I were both hurting. It had been that way for years. I had managed by living in a constant state of masking a lot of feelings. She had simply endured.

It doesn't matter who, when, or how it all happened. Giving airtime to the exclamation mark of it all gets us nowhere. What does matter is the effect it had on me. The pain. The beliefs I carried about myself after it. That's what shaped me.

I lived with the secret as though it were a slow-growing cancer. As an adult, I displayed the textbook symptoms of someone who had been abused: fear, shame, guilt, self-blame, perfectionism, people-pleasing, nightmares. I checked nearly every box.

Two dialectical moments defined my young life in opposite ways. Having Norman Lear cast me in *One Day at a Time* changed me forever in a beautiful way. Being sexually assaulted as a child changed me forever in a devastating one. I developed tools that let me get through life—and while I appreciate the way those tools helped me cope and even succeed, I also see the way they harmed me.

My father, who had his own secrets, wanted everyone to love him. He expected me to be just like him. My mother, though, carried shadows that I've come to recognize. I suspect she'd been assaulted as a young girl. She never said the words outright but hinted enough that I believed it. She taught me, in her silence, to hold it in. Don't bother anyone. Don't deal. Just forget it happened.

No one knew the secret I kept, or how it wove through my marriages and divorces, my body dysmorphia, my decades of dieting, weight gain and loss, buried emotions, my impostor syndrome. My wall was higher and thicker than the barbed wire fence I put up around my house.

There is so much we don't see in each other until it explodes and leaves shrapnel everywhere. Until that happens, we bury it. The friend whose smile seems fake? It's probably a cover-up for shame. The person you know who seems perfect may be desperate to reveal their many imperfections so they can finally breathe. A friend of mine always responds to rudeness with one question: "Who hurt you?"

I think we are supposed to love each other. At the very least, we're supposed to have each other's backs. But too often we honk, flip each other off, or ghost. We vanish. The worst response to evil is indifference; the most harmful response to someone in pain is to ignore them. Worst of all is when we ghost ourselves, as I did for years—ignoring our deepest, darkest wounds under the guise of strength.

* * *

Years ago, I told my therapist that I loved my life even though some terrible things had happened. When she asked me to list them, I mentioned my father's temper and described the time he burst into my bedroom and knocked over my dresser. I also told her about the time my mother threw an Etch A Sketch at me. She probed further. Was there more?

I shook my head. I lied. "Maybe there was more, but I can't remember."

But of course, there was more. And of course, I remembered. How could I forget? I buried it deep down, as far as possible, convinced there was no point in dredging it up. Thinking about it only multiplied the shame. When it managed to work its way into my thoughts, I summoned the strength to push it down again. Why hold on to those feelings? Something terrible had happened and I wanted to forget about it.

Like Scarlett O'Hara, I told myself, "I'll think about it tomorrow." But tomorrow never came. I kept putting it off. By the time I turned sixty, I had accumulated nearly twenty thousand tomorrows. Still, the memory remained, metastasizing like a shadow across my life.

I was plagued by trust issues—I second-guessed myself when I didn't need to and doubted others without reason. I was always bracing for the inevitable release, the explosion. Could I continue to hold it in? And for how long?

Then the dreams began.

In them, the house of my childhood had an upper floor—maybe a second or third story—that I dreaded. A hallway stretched ahead with doors I refused to open. I almost always turned back before reaching the top step. A few times I made it down the hallway. The fear was suffocating. Gasping for breath, I raced back down the stairs and outside to safety.

That's when I woke up.

For decades, I told no one. Even in therapy I stuck to my story. *I love my life. Shitty things happened. But I love my life.*

During my second marriage, I started to gain back the weight I'd lost the past eight or nine years. With it came anger, which was out of character for me. I simmered constantly. Suppressed it. It didn't make sense.

I loved my life, yet I didn't like me.

* * *

Cooking, unlike trauma, made sense to me. You're given the ingredients, and if you follow the recipe, you know the outcome: something delicious. Even when you improvise—adding dried cherries instead of raisins—the lessons are clear. Does it taste good? Wonderful! Too sweet? Try something different next time. As master chef Jacques Pépin said, "There's no failure. You eat your mistakes and try again."

My therapist pressed gently. "Why do you think you're angry?"

I'm sure she saw the signs of abuse and decided to keep prodding until I was ready. For months, we discussed anger, directly and indirectly, circling what both of us either knew or sensed was the truth. Finally, she asked, "Who are you most angry at?"

"Myself," I whispered.

"Why?"

"The shame. The fear. I don't want to hurt anyone."

"Who would get hurt?"

My eyes were shut. I looked like I was saying a prayer. I think I was. Then the words came. "I was sexually abused when I was eleven years old."

Saying it that first time didn't lift a weight. It didn't bring clarity. It didn't immediately heal the wound. What I felt most was the conflict and struggle I'd waged all these years keeping it to myself. And guilt. More than anything. Guilt for speaking it aloud at all.

The fear had always been this: If people knew everything, they wouldn't love me. I would be unlovable. And if not love, what is there?

* * *

Once I spoke the truth, though, I found resolve. I was determined to dig myself out of the shame. I was too old to live this way anymore. I really did want to love my life, the time I had left. It was no longer about denial—it was about rescue.

I knew I had to go back to that room to save the little girl I had once been. But I always chickened out. Still, in all these years, she didn't go away, and neither did the trauma.

"She has no reason to trust me. To tell me what happened to her," I told my therapist.

"She does trust you," my therapist said.

"Why?"

"She loves you."

It was the hardest therapy session of my life. Back in my safe room, I needed all my strength to open the heavy door. There she was, as I'd left her, in her nightgown, eyes full of hope.

"Hi," I said.

"I had a bad dream," she said.

"It wasn't a dream."

I sat down beside her.

"I'm so sorry. We can talk about it if you want, or I can just sit here with you. But I promise you, I won't let it happen again."

Through the calming pulse of the EMDR therapy machine in my hands, I retraced that night five decades earlier. Forty-five minutes went by; it felt like five. I talked the whole time. Walking myself through a horrible night five decades earlier. I kept my eyes closed until the end of the session.

When I finally opened them, tears gushed out like a dam breaking, along with a fragile sense of relief.

* * *

Elie Wiesel—the Holocaust survivor, writer, and Nobel laureate, whose work explored suffering, evil, faith, and hope—often said his two favorite words were "and yet," words that spoke to resilience, to hope, to the possibility of light no matter how dark the night.

The abuse happened—*and yet* I'm still here. It brought pain, anger, embarrassment, guilt, and shame—*and yet* I have known connection, joy, and love. I carry scars—*and yet* I heal again and again.

I used to believe healing meant letting go, purging the pain. Now I know healing is not erasure. It's a reckoning. A settlement of a long-held secret account. An acceptance. An embrace of the whole story—ugly, beautiful, human. A refusal to let shame hold more weight than love.

Because, in the end, healing is about love. It is love. And with love, there is no *and yet*. There is only love.

healing (a meditation)

When we replace judgment with curiosity
our perspective changes
and we can give grace to ourselves and
have empathy for others

JOURNAL ENTRY, MAY 2025

What does it feel like to heal?

It starts with letting yourself feel everything—joy, happiness, grief, regret, anger, fear, pain, relief, exhaustion, enervation, and . . . the whole bundle of emotions that is being human.

Denial is not a part of healing. You know when you're hurting. You know the secrets you are keeping. You know the loss you are feeling. You know the dark rooms that exist in your head and your heart.

Healing requires opening the door to those dark rooms and letting the light in.

"Meet them at the door laughing, and invite them in," as Rumi wrote, noting that all experiences—even painful or difficult ones—should be met with gratitude, as they hold insight into our growth.

Healing requires honesty and vulnerability. It insists you face your pain, loss, regret, sorrow, insecurity, and shame.

Healing involves tears, many tears, enough to cleanse your soul.

Even when you're going through challenging times, sitting through discomfort, and crying. Sometimes sobbing and heaving your way through long-buried trauma, or anger so deep it causes your bones to ache, allows you to be grateful that you're feeling anything at all.

What does it feel like to heal?

You feel a subtle shift and change. You feel a slight movement. You find yourself separating from the harm inflicted on you. You take a step away, maybe two. Sometimes a step back. You feel able to manage the anger, the pain, the shame.

It becomes a part of you but not all of you.

It can sit next to you without hurting you.

You see those individuals from a different angle: If they knew better, they would have done better. And when you know better, you will do better, too.

You gain perspective—for them and yourself.

You won't always see it at the start or in the moment, but it's there when you turn around and look back.

Instead of "Ouch," you say, "Huh?" (That's your curiosity, not your judgment.)

Instead of weight, you feel lightness.

You feel growth, a flowering of your spirit.

What does it feel like to heal?

I feel less anger and hate and so much more compassion and empathy.

I know what it feels like to be in uncomfortable places.

I know that I am no longer there.

What does it feel like to heal?

You feel what it's like to be in uncomfortable places and you know those emotions won't destroy you.

You feel without being afraid to feel.

You feel your whole life rather than feel one thing or one person.

What does it feel like to heal?

Like a warm breeze except there is no breeze. But something feels different. You stop and ask what is that?

It is acceptance.

It is strength.

It is you no longer holding your breath but filling your lungs instead.

It is a deep inhale.

And exhale.

It is life.

What does it feel like to heal?

It feels good.

time

(don't hurry, be happy)

Remember this, this pure, simple, beautiful, nothing day. Today is the day you didn't wear your watch and never asked, "What time is it?" Today is the day you listened to the birds and learned a new song. Today is the day you sat beside that big old tree and said, "Teach me."

JOURNAL ENTRY, MAY 2025

I WAS IN my car, speeding toward Chula Vista, a city near San Diego, from my home in Los Angeles. Yes, I was speeding. Don't tell anyone. Doing seventy-five miles an hour, sometimes eighty-five, despite a designated speed limit of sixty-five. I saw the signs. I blew right past them. I wasn't driving recklessly. Just fast. I couldn't help it. The freeway was wide open, and had I been pulled over, I would've explained to the cop that no, I wasn't late or in a hurry or running behind schedule or anything like that. I was on my way to see my son's band play and listening to his new album, only two songs of which had been released so far, and its hard-driving beat, like it or not, had me pushing hard on the accelerator. Mama Wolf was rockin' out.

Maybe, in addition to the carpool lane, there should be a separate lane for metalheads and hard rockers. Instead of those Clean Air decals you put on cars in California, you'd have a sticker of Ed or Ozzy. Just a suggestion.

I had the volume cranked, especially on the fifth cut, "I Really Wanna," whose chorus I sang at a volume that was even louder than what was coming out of the speakers—which was already pretty damn loud. But hey, when I'm behind the wheel, and by myself, I'm the lead singer. I was having a good . . . time.

The drive south was gorgeous and dramatic. Ocean views. Surfers.[*] A nuclear power plant. Camp Pendleton. More ocean. I was in my own little bubble, racing through Southern California and letting my mind drift and wander until it caught on a rock. That rock was the concept of time.

I'm not going to pretend I'm like Einstein and understand his

---

[*] As fancy and tech-driven as our world has become, I am comforted by the sight of long-haired, suntanned kids driving an old VW van loaded with surfboards. *Hang loose forever!*

theory that time is relative depending on a lot of things I never studied and probably can't explain. But I do know this: When I was in my thirties and driving carpools, my forties making TV movies, and my fifties working on *Hot in Cleveland*, I would often look at my watch, see it was 7 p.m., and wonder where the day went. Now, at sixty-five, I catch myself wondering where the years went. I guess it's all relative, as old Albert claimed.

Perhaps I understand more about time than I give myself credit for. We're obsessed with it. Pay attention to the time. Be on time. Use your time wisely. Get the most out of life before your time is up. Here's the range of my expertise on the subject: When I do laundry, the wash cycle is fifty-three minutes. Leftover steak from a girls' night out can be kept in the fridge for about three days.* Fresh-cut flowers—four, maybe five, unless I forget to change the water. Lemons from my tree, two weeks. I have not had a drink for nearly two years. My son turned thirty-four this year. I turned sixty-five. Ed was sixty-five when he passed. Betty White made it to ninety-nine. Blink and an entire century folds in on itself.

The theme from the movie *Brian's Song*? "The Hands of Time." Cyndi Lauper? "Time After Time." Charles Dickens opened *A Tale of Two Cities* with "It was the best of times, it was the worst of times." The Apollo astronauts took three days to reach the moon; now you can get to the International Space Station in four hours. My drive to Chula Vista took three hours, and I would have happily driven four.

Because then my son and his band, Mammoth, took the stage—and time stopped. Really stopped. That's the magic of a good show, not just Wolfie's show but a movie, a hike, line dancing, or a concert—

---

* Reheated the next day, it's divine, sometimes better than when it's served straight from the restaurant kitchen.

anything that rips you from the clock and drops you into a place where your body moves without permission and your mind feels lighter and free to wander, which was happening to me at the show.

I wished Ed had been there with me. I watched with a girlfriend and my brother, but it wasn't the same. That was our kid onstage. Playing guitar. Singing songs he wrote. I needed an arm to grab. Parents will know what I mean. Ed was the only one who would have understood the way I felt. We would've been competing to see who could whistle the loudest. I remembered Wolfie as a toddler, crawling across the floor to strum one of Ed's guitars. There were guitars throughout the house. Two pianos. A drum set upstairs. Wolfie played them all.

His fingers moved in his sleep like he was already playing. Ed's did the same. As Wolfie got older, he drummed his hands on everything. Music lived in him. It was in his blood, something he and his dad shared. And now he was doing it in front of thousands of people.

Then Wolfie's show was over. Too fast. Where did the time go?

* * *

Only children and fools waste time. Children get a pass if someone teaches them that boredom is an opportunity, not a lifestyle. Fools? They should know better. Though I almost joined them the night I watched Taylor Swift on Travis and Jason Kelce's *New Heights* podcast—the first podcast I'd ever watched from start to finish.

It was two hours long, so I was tempted to fast-forward to the parts that I'd read about, but then I said to myself, "Wait a minute. This is stuff she's never said before. Take it all in. Stop rushing to get to the so-called good part. The whole thing is the good part." Ain't that the truth! The good, the bad, the boring, the heartbreaking, the breathtaking—it's all the good part. Don't skip a minute.

Of course, this wasn't the first time Taylor had reminded me of something important. I had two main takeaways from the podcast. First, her fiancé, Travis Kelce, had clearly heard her yet-to-be-released new album, *The Life of a Showgirl*, and he loved it. He knew it was great, and he was savoring it for a few more months before she shared it with the world. I saw all that in his eyes.

It was the same look I had when I thought about Wolfie's album. It was not scheduled for release for several more months, but I had the entire thing on my computer and my phone and I played it nonstop. Two singles had already been released, and they had millions of views. The next was coming out in a few weeks, and I had told all my friends about it. It was so good, and the video was hilarious. Wolfie being his funny, goofy self. I couldn't wait. But then, seeing that look in Travis's eyes, I thought, "Yes, you can wait. Just enjoy it. Stop rushing."

My other main takeaway from the podcast? I saw a young woman who was so, so, so very much in love. I was envious. But in the best way. I could've watched the podcast just to enjoy the way she looked at him (and he at her), the sparkle in her eyes, the joy radiating from her smile. And the comfort, ease, and contentment between the two of them. Real love. A calm, safe love. I wanted that at least once more in my life. It's all the good part, but that kind of love, it's the best. It's miraculous. I hoped there was still time for me.

I went to the Hollywood Bowl with my friend Beth and her husband to hear the LA Philharmonic perform Gustav Holst's *The Planets*, a seven-movement suite that I read was inspired by astrology. Naturally, I did some stargazing, wondering what they held for me.

Beth said listening to the Los Angeles Philharmonic orchestra at the Bowl was her indulgence, her way of holding on to time, savoring it.

"It moves too quickly," she explained. "It's too hard to take everything in. Here, I can slow it down."

She lets the music pull her into memories—her parents, her childhood, the smell of summer nights—while she travels through time, her thoughts drifting from her classroom earlier in the day to a conversation with her parents decades ago to the arrival of her grandchildren to a Girl Scouts camping trip when she was ten to marveling that she now has three siblings ages seventy or older. She sips wine under stars that are millions of years old and doesn't rush through a second of it.

"I relax," she said. "I reflect. I feel the awesomeness of it all. I take another sip of wine. I fill up with gratitude. I am not in a hurry. I'm just happy."

* * *

Another friend once told me that our lives, relative to the age of the Earth, last the equivalent of two hours and thirty-seven minutes. In the long arc of existence, that's the amount of time each of us is here for. On average. Ed didn't get enough time. Most people don't. Realizing our time is finite should make you think about how you spend what you have. If you only had two hours and thirty-seven minutes to live, how would you spend it?

Definitely not giving the middle finger to people who cut in front of me on the freeway. Let them stew in their own karma. I appreciate my minutes in a way I never did before. Why waste a single one?

One of the reasons I bought my house is the oak tree in the backyard. It's huge, older than my great-grandparents would be now. It stands a couple of hundred feet tall, with thick, gnarled branches that seem to go on forever. It shelters birds, squirrels, and raccoons. Coyotes sneak into the yard behind it. I imagine what it's seen, the storms it's survived.

The tree has a spirit, a sense of divinity, as does all of nature. I feel it when I'm in its presence. Looking out my windows, I sense it, but the feeling is different when I'm near the tree, like being around a holy person, a mystic, a wise teacher. This is why I'm drawn to it. What it knows, its knotted wisdom. It understands time in a way I never will. It doesn't hurry. It just stands, grows, shelters, replenishes, and endures. I visit it when I have questions. I wrap my arms around its trunk as best I can and say hello. I say I love you. I tell it my secrets, my joys. I hope it sees me. I hope it feels like I'm worthy of its companionship. Am I a good caretaker? Am I measuring up? Are you happy here?

It sings its songs to me, its symphonies of rustling leaves and gentle quiet. It responds to my questions with silence, allowing me to hear the voice in me, the voice that if I'm quiet, always knows the answer, always knows the truth. It lets me think. It lets me clear out my thoughts if that's what I need to do. It lets me see where I am rooted, within myself, within my humanity.

It reminds me that I see and feel all that life has to give. The imperfect perfection of my humanity, everything that has brought me to this moment in time, as I suppose it was always meant to be. It tells me to be still. To be present. To wrap my arms around this time, whatever this time may be. Cry. Laugh. Ponder. Wonder. Breathe.

Sit here with me, the tree tells me. *Sit quietly within time, as I have always done. Be grateful for your time.*

Time is all we really have. That and love.

Don't hurry. Be happy.

good work

"Just get up in the morning, look in the mirror, and say, 'I love you.'"
—LOUISE HAY

JOURNAL ENTRY, FEBRUARY 2025

I WAS WISHING my dad were here today. He was a man of many rules, and as you already know, the one he was most passionate about was making sure everybody liked me. *Learn everyone's name*, he told me. *Be nice. Say thank you.* To this day, I can feel my insides curdle if someone thinks poorly of me.

I can't imagine why anyone would. I guess I may not be their cup of tea. They may not want to be around me. They may consider me too loud or not as funny as I think I am or dislike the way I dress or do my hair. They may hate my politics. They may believe I broke up Van Halen.

I don't know. I guess it's easy to find something to dislike about someone else when you go looking for it.

But I wish I could ask my dad how to respond to a recent email I got after I did an interview about my continuing efforts to heal. It said, "Watching you go full fraud is the saddest thing ever. What a waste." When I read the words, I lost my breath for a moment. Then I thought, "Au contraire." The saddest thing ever might be sending an email like that, an email whose sole purpose is to hurt. To me, that's evil.

Isn't there enough evil in the world? The question isn't just "Who hurt you?" It's also "Why are you stopping your day and going out of your way in an attempt to hurt someone?"

I know how the conversation would go with my dad if I showed him that email. He would start by blaming me for opening up publicly about my personal journey, but then he'd turn into my dad.

If they don't like you, screw them; they don't know you.

That's really the lesson I wish he'd taught me. Not everyone is going to like you, and that's okay.

It's just taken me sixty-five years to get to the place where I can accept that. Better late than never.

I've spent the past twenty years trying to move away from hurt and toward love. It sounds like it should be easy. It's not. It's like a difficult ropes course, with challenges and obstacles that must be met and overcome. In order to move forward, you must confront your fears and summon untapped reserves of courage and strength. At the finish line, you feel more confident, like you can do anything.

I have never done a ropes course. I don't think I have the upper body strength. But I have worked on myself, confronted my demons and shadows, cried not merely a river but an ocean. One of my daily horoscopes offered an accurate summation: "You may not see it today or tomorrow, but eventually all of the pieces will add up and bring you somewhere wonderful, or where you always wanted to be. You will be grateful that some things did not work out the way you once wanted them to."

I was having coffee with a friend of mine who is an avid reader with wide and varied tastes, and a soft spot for a good romance. He's a dude who tears up when the boy and girl find each other. He thinks Erich Segal's *Love Story* is the greatest novel ever written. "One hundred and thirty-one pages of perfection," he says, "starting with the first sentences: 'What can you say about a twenty-five-year-old girl who died? That she was beautiful. And brilliant. That she loved Mozart and Bach. And the Beatles. And me.'" He always adds, "The book was so good they released it on the only possible day that made sense, Valentine's Day!"

I swear he tears up talking about it. He also collects Nicholas Sparks first editions and recalls doing a book report in junior high on

Danielle Steel's book *The Promise* when all his classmates were writing about *Lord of the Flies* and *Animal Farm*. His explanation for his taste in literature? "I love love."

So now you know he's kind of a sap. Anyway, we were having coffee and he brought up an interesting question that another favorite author of his posted on social media: Which part of your life would you want someone to be introduced to as the best version of you?

"Right now," I immediately blurted.

My friend said, "About twenty-three years ago."

"Why?"

"I was eleven pounds lighter. My clothes fit. When I sat down, I didn't have an unsightly little pooch."

"It was abs of steel then?"

"Abs-olutely," he said, grinning.

"My friend, you have work to do."

"Duh."

* * *

We laughed, but I went away wondering if I had been too quick to say my best self was right now. I had no reason to doubt it. I just hadn't thought about it. I hadn't thought about why—why was right now my best self? I mean, I was pretty cute and happy when I was eight years old. I don't recall having incurred any psychic wounds or insecurities yet. But I can't say that was my best self. I was only beginning to form as a person. Self-awareness was pretty much limited to deciding whether to put my hair in a ponytail or pull it back with barrettes like

Susan Dey on *The Partridge Family* and wishing I could wiggle my nose like Samantha on *Bewitched*.

When I started work on *One Day at a Time*, I knew it would be a special time in my life, but I didn't realize how extraordinary until the gift of time enabled me to look back with the perspective of adulthood. I was learning how to be an actor. I was learning the magic of comedy. I was learning how to socialize with people older than me. I was learning how to be an individual. I started that show a virgin in every sense of the word and ended it a married woman!

I experienced a huge amount of growth, but I also carried within me an equally huge amount of insecurity. I had no sense of my value as a human being—none whatsoever. I did what I was told and let that be enough. Fame took my anonymity and warped my view not of the world but of myself. The more famous I got, the less I knew myself.

After the show ended, I spent ten years running away from myself. There were drugs. There was alcohol. There were late nights waning into dawn when I dreaded hearing birds chirping.

When I think back on those years, I see myself in full flight. I was in pain. I didn't like anything about myself because I wasn't looking at myself. I couldn't hear my inner voice because I didn't think I had a voice. I saw the way people viewed me. I saw the way people judged me. I saw myself only through other people's eyes, and there were a lot of eyes on me, a lot of voices talking about me, and a lot of judgment. *You're beautiful. You're fat. You're fabulous. You're ugly. You're smart. You're stupid.* I didn't know who to believe, so I believed everyone.

How do you take an honest, unvarnished look at yourself? How do you come out of hiding? Either you recognize the need for self-reflection, or as I think happens to most of us, something forces you to stop—and when you do, it usually isn't a big pile of roses you smell, I can tell you that.

* * *

If you're lucky, one day you find what's been missing—a life that gives you satisfaction and makes you happy.

When your life falls apart or gets so bad that it feels unmanageable, you get to put the pieces back together, and in doing so, you are able to find your true self. You get to confront your life—secrets, regrets, mistakes, the good, the bad, and the parts you wish had never happened. In recovery programs, they call this making an honest and uncompromising personal inventory. I call it simply telling the truth and doing the work—the good work.

I was thirty years old when I gave birth to my son, Wolfie. All through my pregnancy and from the day he arrived, I felt like I had found what I was here to do—be a mom and care for my son. I want to say I loved every minute of it, but I loved most minutes of it. There were challenges, and fears, but the unconditional love and joy I felt raising him became my drug of choice. I found compassion and empathy for my son and others. It was, as I say, good work.

But was it the best of me? Answering yes to that question would be the easy way out. I'd have to call BS on myself. I'm wiser than that now.

The truth is, raising Wolfie was where some of the good work took place, but this recent journey was the hard work, the painful work. I had to learn to acknowledge that I had to have compassion and empathy *for myself*. I had to understand and ameliorate the self-hate and shame that was so much a part of me, and the better I got at that, the more of me I could give to others. Now, that's the *real* good work.

Two divorces, an unhealthy obsession with weight and body image, getting fired, and turning sixty will do that to you. Seriously. It was not a wake-up call. It was a freaking loud smoke detector going off in the middle of the night, screaming: *At best you have twentysomething years left. What are you doing with the rest of your life? Start making it matter right now!*

And I did. I have. Which is why I wouldn't pick any of those years, even those during peak mommyhood, as the best of me.

* * *

I flew back to New York at the beginning of April with two VIP companions: a pink stuffed bear and an E.T. doll. Both had belonged to Drew Barrymore when she was a child. She had given them to a friend of mine when she was a teenager, and his daughters had played with them. Now his daughters were adults, and the bear and the doll had kept each other company on a closet shelf for the past thirty years.

Somehow my friend heard that Drew had mentioned she didn't have many things from her childhood, and soon the bear and the doll showed up at my house, ready to jet across the country and return to their rightful owner. When I gave them to Drew backstage at the show, she stared spellbound at them, especially the pink bear.

"She's going on my bed tonight," she said.

I mention this not to exploit a private moment but instead because of the way Drew looked at that bear. It stayed with me. I knew that look. It occurs when something or someone unexpectedly appears in front of you and becomes a window into the past. You look as hard as you can and sometimes you can go back. Sometimes you're blocked, you can't get there. When that happens, it's usually because you're not ready.

I have looked back at my two marriages, at my parents, at my own parenting, at my career choices, asking myself why I made certain decisions, what compelled me to do or say various things. Sometimes I can see all the way back, other times I am peeking around corners, and sometimes I find answers to my questions.

After more than fifty years in the public eye, I've accumulated some real cringe moments. But that doesn't mean they're bad or things I should regret. There is strength in revealing yourself, your truths. There is *revelation*. You have to love yourself anyway.

That's the work we have to do, that I've done and I'm still doing. The hard work. The good work.

After giving Drew those stuffed cuties from her childhood, I had the next day off. It was raining but I ventured out in the city anyway. I found myself at the Hayden Planetarium, which is part of the American Museum of Natural History at Seventy-Seventh Street and Central Park West.

I took a seat in the planetarium's theater and had my mind blown by the space show, an immersive "journey far beyond our own blue planet." Seeing our beautiful planet sitting in space had the intended effect: I was overwhelmed by the humbling miracle that is us, our brief flicker of existence in this vast, inexplicable universe of hot gas, cold darkness, and stardust.

Afterward I headed back out into the rain, and because there were no roses to smell in the park, I headed to Nordstrom to put my nose on some new perfume I wanted. I caught sight of myself in the mirror and paused to look. I can't begin to estimate the number of hours I have spent looking at myself in the mirror at work, and I can say with certainty that after a while, indeed after years, sometimes I don't see anything but a blank canvas for the makeup artists to do their thing.

This time, though, as I looked at myself in that square mirror on the counter, I saw layers of myself. It was almost the same effect I'd seen at the planetarium. I could see youth in my face, my younger self, and I could remember the way I used to look at myself, searching for flaws and ways I could fix them. I practiced looks. I tried on smiles as I looked for this person everyone seemed to like except me.

But then I also saw myself in the present. I saw the wrinkles and the lines, all sixtysomething years. I saw wisdom in my eyes, and more confidence than self-doubt. I smiled—my smile. I liked this person and didn't worry about what other people thought.

"Can I help you?" the woman behind the counter asked.

I almost laughed. Talk about a loaded question.

"No thanks," I said. "I'm good."

Good is not an end point, of course. There is no saying I'm done. I'm not saying I'm *there*. I don't know if I'll ever be there. I don't know if there is a there *there*. We're all always striving to do better, to learn, to grow, to heal, to love.

Later that week I got out my journal and wrote:

I wouldn't be who or where I am today without going through all the shit and doing all the work. It's what made me who I am today. Bad shit happens to everyone. Only some of us acknowledge it, deal with it, and know we don't have to be prisoner to it. We can get to the other side of it. We can get better. We can understand. Though sometimes it won't be something that's understandable. It will just be a lesson in perseverance and honesty, grit and a desire to feel more love than pain. You can't feel bliss without also knowing struggle and shame. Healing is hard work. It takes the time it takes. But the rewards are worth it. I find myself looking up and saying thank you so often I wonder if I have turned into a crazy zealot who thinks they have a direct line to the Almighty. I purr with gratitude. I feel solid and strong, like the bad stuff didn't hurt me, didn't kill me, it helped—or forced me to help myself. I am going into this stage feeling like

I deserve to feel good and have good people in my life and have good things happen. I look forward to those moments of peacefulness and grace. I acknowledge them. I look forward to waking up and hearing the birds chirp. I say, "Hey, thanks for showing up." I say that to myself now. Hey, thanks for showing up.

When faced with a choice, choose to do the work. Choose happy. Choose love. Choose gratitude. Choose to say thank you.

a parting thought

"We're gone in a blizzard of seconds.
Love the body human while we're here. . . .
Give thanks or go home a waste of spark."
—MARTY MCCONNELL, "INSTRUCTIONS FOR A BODY"

JOURNAL ENTRY, MAY 2025

I WAS UP late last night at my son's house, where I got a new tattoo on my arm—a tiny image of Earth, our home. I have a quarter moon in the same place on my other forearm. The meaning of both? I love Wolf to the moon and back. I've said this to him since he arrived in this world.

My days as a rock and roll mama are mostly behind me, so it was way past my normal bedtime when I got home. Luna and I walked into the house and were met at the door by Batman and Tigger. They were pissed—the before-bed treats were far beyond late. Henry, Beau, and Bubba were roaming the kitchen waiting patiently.

"I'm so sorry, boys. I was at Wolfie's. Treats are coming!" I said.

As soon as we all climbed into bed, I was asleep and off in dreamland. Literally. I pictured myself at my brother David's house. He and his family live in the Midwest, where he's an animal control officer. He rescues furry and feathered creatures every day. I wanted to do something nice for him. I suggested cleaning his house as a surprise to his wife.

He had something else in mind. Painting his house. He grabbed a brush and got to work. I picked up a brush and joined him. We didn't stop until we'd painted the entire house. Both of us were totally exhausted.

I woke up feeling the same way, like I'd worked all night, except it was a good kind of tired. A little stretch in the sun and a strong cup of coffee helped refresh me. I couldn't shake the dream I'd had and didn't know if I wanted to. It had felt so good while I was in it. Now, in the light of day, I wanted to know what it meant.

A few computer clicks on the Google later, I learned that painting someone's house "can symbolize a few things, including bonding, self-expression, and a desire to make a positive change. It can also represent the effort and dedication needed to create a life that feels like a masterpiece." I liked that interpretation. *To create a life that feels like a masterpiece.* It was a lofty goal. It made sense, more than ever, at my age. How much time did I have left? Why aim for anything less?

That's my advice to others. Create your own masterpiece. If you're like me, and I always suspect we're more alike than we realize, you've been doing the work for much of your life. Sometimes without even knowing it. You've seen results but know there's more work to do. You may not be able to articulate it, but you sense it. Or you know exactly what it is you need to address but have labeled it unspeakable. To you, I say, "Be patient with yourself. Be kind. Be strong. And be courageous." You will get there. It takes time—in my case, it's taken decades. And I'm still working at it.

Recently I opened one of my journals and found this entry:

> Writer Alan Watts has a theory called the "backwards law" that says accepting negative experiences can be a positive experience. The more you strive to avoid the negative ones, the less satisfied you actually become. Acceptance is a state of happiness. Acceptance for whatever state you're in instead of looking for happiness. Acceptance for whatever you're feeling leads to more peace. Accept where you are and be grateful. So, then, accepting the shitty stuff in and of itself becomes a positive experience!

Amen.

In September 2025, I did something outlandishly positive. I treated myself to a jaunt to Paris with girlfriends. I never would've let myself feel deserving of such an indulgent excursion before, but when I bit into the first of many fresh croissants on that trip, while sitting in a cute café watching *tout le monde* pass by, I pinched myself and said, "Yes." For too many years, I had normalized and gotten so used to living in emotional discomfort that this unadulterated joy felt odd. It felt exhilarating and unfamiliar yet still somehow mine, like a beloved pet that had gone missing for years and found its way back into my arms.

One day as I walked through the Marais, I was thinking about how much I love this feeling, and although I am and will always be grateful for the lessons that I have learned through all the painful stuff, I would like to ease out of that particular educational institution, please and thank you. I began silently chanting a mantra: "Teach me through patience and peace, not pain. I'm listening now." Soon I started to find all sorts of feathers in my path. I barely noticed the first one. By the fifth or sixth, I was curious. "They're signs," one of my girlfriends said. "Sent by your angels."

OK, fine. Who would argue with that? Certainly not *moi*. But of course I had to get on the Google. And indeed, the spiritual interpretation is that feathers are a wink from the universe. White feathers are most often linked to angels and peace. All the feathers I had found were gray with black and white or all gray. Not white. Back home in LA, I kept chanting. "Teach me through patience and peace, not pain. I'm listening." A few weeks later, I went to New York City for *The Drew Barrymore Show*. Whenever I thought about it, I would chant those lines to myself. On the plane, in the car that took me to my hotel, waiting at the check-in desk, and so on. I thought it was working. If you put out that vibe, you get it back, and between Drew and Ross and the show's crew, I was swimming in good, positive vibes. But the feather thing puzzled me. Was it a phenomenon? Or was it a freaky coincidence?

I proposed a test. While walking the half mile back to my hotel after a day on the set, I stopped at Tenth Avenue and Fifty-Seventh Street, I looked up into the sky and said, "I want to see a white feather." Not a dirty New York City pigeon feather. A pristine white feather. And I wanted to see it before I got to my hotel. What were the odds of that happening on one of the most trafficked sidewalks in all of Manhattan? I should've bought a lottery ticket, because before I hit Ninth Avenue, before I finished chanting "Teach me through patience and peace, not pain," I looked down and spotted—that's right—a white feather. I stopped. I gasped. "Come on." I picked up the feather. I looked at it, amazed and impressed. My angels. I smiled and turned my gaze toward the heavens. "Thank you, universe!"

* * *

It took me a long time to figure out everything I've shared in these stories, but once I did, I realized the bad stuff is losing its power over me. I not only survived it, I love my life even more. So get naked. Do the hard work. Go to those dark places. Fearlessly. Without shame. And from a place of love. Free yourself. Feel your power. Let the light in. Live in peace, not pain. I know it ain't easy. But if I can do it, you can, too. Get help if you can. Surround yourself with people who support you. Be courageous. Be kind to yourself. One day you'll realize, as I have, that you are and always have been imperfectly perfect, a masterpiece.

To the moon and back,

Val

acknowledgments

I'LL TELL YOU what: It's a privilege to say thank you. You're reading this lovely, intensely personal, and beautiful (I think) book, and I am grateful. I appreciate the community that surrounds me at home, on the road, online, at work, on airplanes, at the perfume counter, in the grocery store . . . my menagerie of pets, and all the critters in my yard. I am so thankful for my family and every single one of my girlfriends and their families. I feel the same way about the authors and writers whose books and blogs have opened my eyes and filled my heart and shared insights that have made me think in new ways about this great adventure that is life. Also the therapists, soothsayers, mediums, doctors, angels, and spirits who've told me the right direction is the way I'm going. Bless you. I am grateful for the sun and the moon and this gorgeous, miraculous planet we call home. I know that—or some of it—might sound a little (okay a lot) woo-woo, but it's true. Like it or not, all of us have some woo-woo in us. Some days may be heavy but on most of them, I walk with a lighter step. My daily cup of gratitude runneth over. It's a great way to feel. And I hope to sprinkle that feeling everywhere.

ACKNOWLEDGMENTS

I love this book. I'm proud of it. I feel like I climbed a mountain—the mountain inside me. Maybe several peaks. I often sat by myself in front of my computer in my little upstairs office, but the thing about producing a book is that I was never alone. Everyone I wrote about was with me in one way or another. Friends and followers online offered encouragement and shared their anticipation. And behind the scenes there were smart, talented people ready to make the words I typed on the screen appear on paper, on iPads and Kindles, and in a script I could record for the audiobook. Amazing. I'm humbled, thankful, and happy that all of you were there for me, starting with my longtime managers, Marc Schwartz and Jack Grossbart, and my literary agent, Dan Strone. Seven books over sixteen years? As a girl who didn't graduate high school, I never imagined loving homework this much.

Then there are the smart, talented, hard-working people at Harvest Books, an imprint of HarperCollins Publishers: my brilliant editor, Diana Baroni, whose edits and advice began shaping this book way back when I had written only one chapter. The tireless Emma Effinger, associate editor, who kept this book (and me) on track and on time, which is a task and a half; and copy editor Heather Rodino, whose side comments on this and previous books are indispensable and a great read on their own. The rest of the clever, talented team at Harvest who made this book possible include Odette Fleming (marketing), Anwesha Basu (publicity), Mumtaz Mustafa (cover designer), and Hope Breeman (production editor). Beautiful names, beautiful people, beautiful job. Thank you and thank you to every single person that works at Harvest and HarperCollins!

Photographer John Russo needs a special paragraph of his own. I mean, I got naked for this shoot. I took my clothes off in front of your camera—and you kept your eyes open while keeping me safe in my vulnerability—and now everyone can see what I found so painful to look at for so much of my life. But no longer. Thank you! I'm so grateful for the team that day and so many other days: Lisa Ashley, Kimmie Urgel, Lori Eskowitz, and Zachary Bradshaw. I love you. Thank you.

Drew, Ross, Jason, and the entire crew—what you're selling, I'm not only buying, I'm doing my best to pass it on. What a legacy you're giving to everyone who watches and I'm so grateful to be a small part of it.

Finally, my friend Todd, our thirty-year-plus friendship means the world to me. You pushed me hard with this book and helped me process things I didn't think possible, and I am eternally grateful. You always know when to make me laugh and when to pass the tissues. It's a wild ride! We'll remember this one. Love you.

Wolfie, thank you for loving me unconditionally. Never in my life have I known what that feels like until you. You are the embodiment of *love is patient, love is kind* . . . I cherish you and Draia, Pat and Stacy, David, Jessica and Enzo, Michael, Launa, and Landon. Love, love, love for all my brothers, friends, and their beautiful wives, husbands, and families.

Love to everyone in and around Mammoth and all the hard work you do to make it so successful. My favorite band!

Just love.

And that brings me to one of the most important points I included in this book. I make it a point to tell people in my life that I love them. I don't say it frivolously. I mean it when I say it. And I say it out loud. I want people to hear it. And now, to all of you who've been with me all these years, please know that I'm with you, too. It's a wonderful, blessed thing. Thank you.

I love you.